Quarterly Essay

1 THE AUSTRALIAN DREAM
Blood, History and Becoming
Stan Grant

83 CORRESPONDENCE
Patrick Lawrence, Nicole Hemmer, Bruce Wolpe, Dennis Altman,
David Goodman, Patrick McCaughey, Gary Werskey, Don Watson

113 Contributors

Quarterly Essay is published four times a year by Black Inc., an imprint of Schwartz Publishing Pty Ltd. Publisher: Morry Schwartz.

ISBN 978-1-86395-889-9 ISSN 1832-0953

Subscriptions – 1 year print & digital
(4 issues): $79.95 within Australia incl. GST. Outside Australia $119.95. 2 years print & digital (8 issues): $129.95 within Australia incl. GST. 1 year digital only: $39.95.

Payment may be made by Mastercard or Visa, or by cheque made out to Schwartz Publishing. Payment includes postage and handling.

To subscribe, fill out and post the subscription card or form inside this issue, or subscribe online:
www.quarterlyessay.com
subscribe@blackincbooks.com
Phone: 61 3 9486 0288

Correspondence should be addressed to:

The Editor, Quarterly Essay
Level 1, 221 Drummond Street
Carlton VIC 3053 Australia
Phone: 61 3 9486 0288 / Fax: 61 3 9011 6106
Email: quarterlyessay@blackincbooks.com

Editor: Chris Feik. Management: Caitlin Yates. Publicity: Anna Lensky. Design: Guy Mirabella. Assistant Editor: Kirstie Innes-Will. Production Coordinator: Siân Scott-Clash. Typesetting: Tristan Main.

Printed in Australia by McPherson's Printing Group. The paper used to produce this book comes from wood grown in sustainable forests.

THE AUSTRALIAN DREAM | Blood, History and Becoming

Stan Grant

"Amid thunder, the golden house of is
Collapses, and the world of becoming ascends."
> — Czesław Miłosz, "A Treatise on Poetry"

"The Dreaming and The Market are mutually exclusive."
> — W.E.H. Stanner, "Continuity and change among the Aborigines"

THE SPEECH

27 October 2015: City Recital Hall, Sydney, New South Wales
"Thank you so much for coming along this evening, and I would also like to extend my respects to my Gadigal brothers and sisters from my people, the Wiradjuri people.

In the winter of 2015, Australia turned to face itself. It looked into its soul and it had to ask this question: who are we? What sort of country do we want to be? And this happened in a place that is most holy, most sacred to Australians. It happened on the sporting field, it happened on the football field. Suddenly the front page was on the back page, it was in the grandstands.

Thousands of voices rose to hound an Indigenous man. A man who was told he wasn't Australian. A man who was told he wasn't Australian of the Year. And they hounded that man into submission.

I can't speak for what lay in the hearts of the people who booed Adam Goodes. But I can tell you what we heard when we heard those boos. We heard a sound that was very familiar to us.

We heard a howl. We heard a howl of humiliation that echoes across two centuries of dispossession, injustice, suffering and survival. We heard the howl of the Australian Dream, and it said to us again: you're not welcome.

The Australian Dream.

We sing of it, and we recite it in verse: 'Australians all, let us rejoice, for we are young and free.'

My people die young in this country. We die ten years younger than average Australians and we are far from free. We are fewer than 3 per cent of the Australian population and yet we are 25 per cent – a quarter of those Australians – locked up in our prisons – and if you are a juvenile, it is worse, it is 50 per cent. An Indigenous child is more likely to be locked up in prison than they are to finish high school.

'I love a sunburned country, a land of sweeping plains, of rugged mountain ranges ...'

It reminds me that my people were killed on those plains. We were shot on those plains, disease ravaged us on those plains.

I come from those plains. I come from a people west of the Blue Mountains – the Wiradjuri people – where in the 1820s the soldiers and settlers waged a war of extermination against my people.

Yes, a war of extermination!

That was the language used at the time. Go to the *Sydney Gazette* and look it up and read about it. Martial law was declared and my people could be shot on sight. Those rugged mountain ranges – my people, women and children, were herded over those ranges to their deaths.

The Australian Dream.

The Australian Dream is rooted in racism. It is the very foundation of the dream. It is there at the birth of the nation. It is there in *terra nullius*. An empty land. A land for the taking. Sixty thousand years of occupation. A people who made the first seafaring journey in the history of mankind. A people of law, a people of lore, a people of music and art and dance and politics. None of it mattered because our rights were extinguished because we were not here according to British law.

And when British people looked at us, they saw something subhuman, and if we were human at all, we occupied the lowest rung on civilisation's ladder. We were flyblown, Stone Age savages, and that was the language that was used. Charles Dickens, the great writer of the age, when referring to the 'noble savage', which we were counted among, said, 'It would be better that they be wiped off the face of the earth.'

Captain Arthur Phillip, a man of enlightenment, a man who was instructed to make peace with the so-called natives in a matter of years, was sending out raiding parties with the instruction, 'Bring back the severed heads of the black troublemakers.'

They were smoothing the dying pillow.

My people were rounded up and put on missions from where, if you escaped, you were hunted down, you were roped and tied and dragged back, and it happened here. It happened on the mission that my grandmother and my great-grandmother are from, the Warangesda on the Darling Point of the Murrumbidgee River.

Read about it. It happened.

By 1901, when we became a nation, when we federated the colonies, we were nowhere. We're not in the Constitution, save for 'race provisions,' which allowed for laws to be made that would take our children, that would invade our privacy, that would tell us who we could marry and tell us where we could live.

The Australian Dream.

By 1963, the year of my birth, the dispossession was continuing. Police came at gunpoint under cover of darkness to Mapoon, an Aboriginal community in Queensland, and they ordered people from their homes and they burned those homes to the ground and they gave the land to a bauxite mining company. And today those people remember that as the 'Night of the Burning.'

In 1963, when I was born, I was counted among the flora and fauna, not among the citizens of this country.

Now, you will hear things tonight. You will hear people say, 'But you've done well.' Yes, I have, and I'm proud of it, and why have I done well? I've done well because of who has come before me. My father, who lost the tips of three fingers working in sawmills to put food on our table because he was denied an education. My grandfather, who served to fight wars for this country when he was not yet a citizen and came back to a segregated land where he couldn't even share a drink with his digger mates in the pub because he was black.

My great-grandfather, who was jailed for speaking his language to his grandson (my father). Jailed for it! My grandfather on my mother's side, who married a white woman, who reached out to Australia, lived on the fringes of town until the police came, put a gun to his head, bulldozed his tin humpy and ran over the graves of the three children he buried there.

That's the Australian Dream.

I have succeeded in spite of the Australian Dream, not because of it, and I've succeeded because of those people.

You might hear tonight, 'But you have white blood in you.' And if the white blood in me was here tonight, my grandmother, she would tell you of how she was turned away from a hospital giving birth to her first child because she was giving birth to the child of a black person.

The Australian Dream.

We're better than this. I have seen the worst of the world as a reporter. I spent a decade in war zones from Iraq to Afghanistan and Pakistan. We are an extraordinary country. We are in so many respects the envy of the world. If I was sitting here where my friends are tonight, I would be arguing passionately for this country. But I stand here with my ancestors, and the view looks very different from where I stand.

The Australian Dream.

We have our heroes. Albert Namatjira painted the soul of this nation. Vincent Lingiari put his hand out for Gough Whitlam to pour the sand of his country through his fingers and say, 'This is my country.' Cathy Freeman lit the torch of the Olympic Games.

But every time we are lured into the light, we are mugged by the darkness of this country's history.

Of course racism is killing the Australian Dream. It is self-evident that it's killing the Australian Dream. But we are better than that.

The people who stood up and supported Adam Goodes and said, 'No more,' they are better than that. The people who marched across the bridge for reconciliation, they are better than that. The people who supported Kevin Rudd when he said sorry to the Stolen Generations, they are better than that. My children and their non-Indigenous friends are better than that. My wife, who is not Indigenous, is better than that.

And one day, I want to stand here and be able to say as proudly and sing as loudly as anyone else in this room, 'Australians all, let us rejoice.'

Thank you."

Washington was snowed in. This was a blizzard of record proportions. The capital was buried under two feet of snow. The mid-Atlantic states had rarely seen anything like it. Television networks were covering the impact around the clock; it was now rated category 4, or a "crippling storm." More than fifty people would be killed and thousands left without power or stranded. I made it out just hours before the airport was shut down. In Australia it was already tomorrow.

Just the day before, I had stood in the Oval Office at the White House, almost close enough to reach out and touch the president of the United States. I was in Washington for Sky News, reporting Prime Minister Malcolm Turnbull's visit to the US. This was familiar territory for me and I was in my element. I relished the long hours and irregular meals, the sleeplessness and constant anxiety of life on the road. The freezing temperatures only added to the excitement. My cameraman and I were working from 7 a.m. to 4 a.m. the following day. This was the curse of the international dateline: night was day and day was night; we were always on deadline. The snow was coming down in sheets so heavy that at times I would vanish from the television screen, a voice lost in a blizzard.

The prime minister and the president were focused on China, the great foreign-policy puzzle of our age. More than anything else – terrorism, Russia, economic crisis – the relationship between the superpower and its emerging rival would determine the course of the twenty-first century. I had lived in and reported on China on and off for a decade – it fascinated and consumed me. Were the two countries on a collision course that would plunge the world into conflict? Certainly, China – rich and power-ful – was making its presence felt, challenging American hegemony. The fault-lines stretched from the islands disputed with Japan to the South China Sea; from the North Korean border to disputed Kashmir, where China faced an old and equally rising foe in India.

Malcolm Turnbull had recently spoken of the "Thucydides trap": a warning from the Peloponnesian War, when a rising Athens had made war with Sparta inevitable. Now China and the United States were in danger of repeating history. Before leaving Washington, I and other reporters quizzed the prime minister at a reception held at the home of the departing Australian ambassador to the United States, Kim Beazley.

World leaders, global events: it was a long way to come for a boy who had lived much of his early life looking out the back window of a car. I had spent my childhood years on the road, as my family moved from town to town searching for work. We were poor, essentially homeless, relying on whatever food my father's muscles could earn, and when that failed on whatever the churches or charities would give us. We were not just poor, we were black: Aborigines – or, as we were more likely to be called then, "Abos." Now, here I was in business class, flying from Washington to Sydney, clutching a book recounting the story of the Obama presidency, relieved I had escaped the blizzard but, unbeknown to me, about to fly into a different kind of storm. A speech I had given months earlier and promptly forgotten had suddenly "gone viral."

Until now, I have never seen the speech written down. I delivered it unrehearsed and unscripted. I wanted it to be immediate and forceful. I wanted to look the audience in the eye and hold them. I didn't want to look down at notes. I didn't need them, for this story I had been told since childhood. It was a story I had reported on as a journalist in faraway countries, in which people felt the sting of invasion and colonisation. It was a "war story," and as the Vietnamese writer and academic Viet Thanh Nguyen, speaking of his own turbulent history, says: "All wars are fought twice, the first time on the battlefield, the second time in memory."

The speech was given as the opening address of a debate, and attracted little comment, but then the Ethics Centre posted the footage on its website. The reaction to and praise for the speech was – all modesty aside – far more than it deserved. It was an accident of timing: it coincided with

Australia Day, a time of reflection and celebration, and, for many Indigenous people, great sadness or anger. The broadcaster and journalist Mike Carlton gave it an extra push. He called it Australia's Martin Luther King moment, referring to the American civil rights leader's "I have a dream" speech.

Noel Pearson, the Indigenous lawyer and activist, in an address to the National Press Club, called my speech a "tour de force." He said it did for black Australia what Prime Minister Paul Keating's Redfern speech in 1992 did for white Australia. At Redfern, Keating laid bare Australia's dark history of frontier wars and stolen children. But the stakes were higher for Keating, speaking as prime minister, than for me. Pearson also reminded us that there was nothing in my speech "unfamiliar to blackfellas." He was right. Pearson himself has spoken powerfully about our history, notably two decades earlier, in a speech to the 1997 Australian Reconciliation Convention in Melbourne:

> It is a troubling business coming to terms with Australian history, both for Aboriginal people and for non-Aboriginal people. For our people it is a troubling business because there is the imperative of never allowing anyone to forget the truths of the past, but being able as a community to rise above its demoralising legacy ... But it's also a challenge for non-Aboriginal Australia. A challenge to understand that in the same way that they urge pride in Gallipoli, and in Kokoda ... can we as a community and a nation also acknowledge the shameful aspects of that same past?

There is, in fact, a long and distinguished history of courage and oratory among Indigenous people. Jack Patten, the first president of the Aborigines' Progressive Association, inaugurated a "Day of Mourning" at the Australian Hall on Elizabeth Street in Sydney on Australia Day, 1938.

> On this day the white people are rejoicing, but we, as Aborigines, have no reason to rejoice on Australia's 150th birthday ... This land

belonged to our forefathers ... Give us the chance! We do not wish to be left behind in Australia's march to progress ... we do not wish to be herded like cattle.

Charles Perkins, Gary Foley, Chicka Dixon, Marcia Langton, Jackie Huggins, Noel Pearson, Michael Mansell and so many others have spoken truth to Australian power. They have argued for the recognition of Indigenous rights, of title to land and the need for self-determination. I happily concede that all have had a greater claim than me to speak for Indigenous people, something I have never wanted to do. Far from being Martin Luther King, I stood on the shoulders of generations of giants.

However worthy my words were, I have lived the past year with their weight. My speech seemingly became all things to all people. Many Indigenous people felt that in telling my family's story, I had told theirs too. Other Australians seized on my belief that we are better than our worst. To some, I may have let white people off the hook, too readily absolved them of their sins. Yet I believe it is possible to speak to a country's shame and still have love for that country. I can no more deny the greatness of Australia as a peaceful, cohesive, prosperous society than my fellow countrymen and women can deny the legacy of neglect and bigotry and injustice that traps so many Indigenous brothers and sisters still.

The journalist Amy McQuire penned an insightful and challenging critique of my speech, entitled "The Viral Rise of Stan Grant: Why Diplomacy Won't Be Enough for Our People." She acknowledged that I had tied the heartache felt by Indigenous people today to the destruction and dispossession from colonisation and assimilation. But, she said, "the fever-pitch around Grant ... says more about the state of the nation than anything he has uttered so far." Australia listened to me, she said, because I am unthreatening and diplomatic. Unlike other Indigenous voices, mine doesn't unsettle white Australia, she said – in fact, my words comfort it.

Yet the so-called "radical" voices McQuire admires have had little trouble being heard and rewarded in Australia. The voice of protest has moved the country; it has changed our law: we are a better country because of those voices. Some of them now enjoy lucrative positions in government and academia. That too says much about the state of the nation.

McQuire's assessment does hold some essential historical truths. Australia has had trouble seeing us except in its own image. But in 2016 we have a place in our country. Indigenous claims can be disputed, but not ignored. Amy McQuire and I have different experiences of the world. I have lived in and reported on countries torn apart by war, where death and suffering are occurring on a catastrophic scale. Whatever our challenges in Australia today, this is not Syria, or Iraq, or Afghanistan. My diplomacy – if that's what it is – is a reflection of the life I have made – the life my parents and grandparents prepared for me. I have moved from the fringes to the centre. I don't want to live in a country fractured by its history. I want to share in a sense of the possibilities of our nation. But nor do I want to live in a country that shrouds its past in silence. I don't want to live in a country where the people who share my heritage, whose ancestry connects to the first footprints on our continent, too often live in misery.

To me, the most important line in my speech was the last: "And one day, I want to stand here and be able to say as proudly and sing as loudly as anyone else in this room, 'Australians all, let us rejoice.'"

This essay seeks to probe that desire. It is in essence a coda to my speech. I wish to answer what may be – for me, at least – the most confronting question of identity: am I Australian? I don't mean by this the facts of my citizenship, my country of birth, my passport, but rather to pose the question in the sense of the philosopher Hegel, who declared, "Man is not at home in the world." Does my history lock me in a perpetual state of existential crisis? Am I bound to remain, as I have written before, estranged in the land of my ancestors? Perhaps I share the fate of the poet Czesław Miłosz, born in Lithuania, a country variously occupied and dominated until its independence in 1990, who said, "I am a Lithuanian to whom it was not given to be a Lithuanian." Am I an Australian to whom it was not given to be an Australian?

This is in part a *cri de coeur*; how could it not be? For _____ year of contemplation, reassessment and revelation. I _____ country, travelling from the biggest cities to the red cent _____ of the north. The journey has involved confronting the b _____ life for many Indigenous people, and wondering how th _____ my life of privilege and whether my place in Australia is a place for us all. In a year of suicide, torture, the screams of black kids behind bars, broken lives and broken faces, deaths in lonely cells, I keep asking: how can this happen in Australia, in a country like this? But it is happening and it keeps happening, to one generation after the next.

In Australian towns right now, children are kept awake by the cries of their mothers being beaten, their fathers locked in a spiral of hopelessness broken only by the relief of grog or drugs. In these Australian towns there are no grandparents; to be forty is to be old. The graveyards are marked with white crosses of lives ended too soon. In these Australian towns kids will not finish high school; they will get their education in a cell. They will more than likely graduate to an adult prison. In these Australian towns people live crowded thirty to a home, with no more privacy than the mangy dogs that share their beds. This is Australia for too many Indigenous people.

This unfolds in a place "out there," somewhere hidden far from view. We speak of these places in terms not of lives lived, but of statistics tallied. We know them so well they have become a mantra: the most disadvantaged; the worst health outcomes; the poorest housing; the least educated; the most incarcerated. Even on this sad balance sheet some numbers are startling: Indigenous people are fewer than 3 per cent of the Australian population, yet comprise more than a quarter of those in prison; black kids make up half the Australians in juvenile detention. In the Northern Territory 97 per cent of children locked up are Indigenous. Indigenous women are over thirty times more likely to suffer domestic violence, and far too often the law does nothing to protect them, and too many Aboriginal men are silent.

Over the course of my life, I have lived some of this, and some in my family continue to live it. This year I have been immersed in these stories and I admit that it has at times laid me low. I have felt a responsibility, but a powerlessness to change anything. I have sometimes felt suffocated by the world of Indigenous affairs, which can be stifling and demoralising. It is too easy to become consumed to the point that one loses all perspective. I remind myself that I have seen suffering on a mind-blowing scale: the slaughter of hundreds of thousands in war, children blown to pieces in terrorist bombings, entire peoples held in totalitarian bondage, thousands of lives lost in a minute by shattering acts of God or nature. I tell myself this not to diminish individual suffering here, but to wonder why it has to continue in a country so much more fortunate than those I have spent my life reporting on.

This essay is not a litany of horrors. We know that story – I have told that story – and for those who don't know it, there are works such as Henry Reynolds' *The Other Side of the Frontier*, Lyndall Ryan's *The Aboriginal Tasmanians* and Rosalind Kidd's *The Way We Civilise*, and the brilliant work of Indigenous writers such as Ellen van Neerven, Anita Heiss, Kim Scott, Alexis Wright and Bruce Pascoe; and there are the heartbreaking songmen: Geoffrey Gurrumul Yunupingu, Frank Yamma, Archie Roach.

But history – the history of dispossession and ensuing suffering – can be an all-too-convenient explanation of what ails us. This year I have had to confront whether I have perpetuated a lazy narrative that obscures a more complete story of the dynamism and potential of Australia and its first peoples. It wasn't my intention, but when I hear how people at all points on the spectrum – black and white, left and right – have interpreted my Australian Dream speech, I fear that has been the outcome. I would hope that the telling of history can connect us, be cathartic and provide a roadmap from our past to our future.

The most confronting but liberating book I read this past year is David Rieff's *In Praise of Forgetting: Historical Memory and Its Ironies*. Rieff, like me, has been a journalist, and the reporting of war and suffering has forced him to challenge the idea that we must hold tight to our histories, lest we forget them. "'Lest we forget,'" he writes, "is a mournful acknowledgment that such forgetting is inevitable ... Thinking about history ... is far more likely to paralyse than encourage and inspire."

But we cling to it anyway, each in our own way, selecting those aspects of the past that we think best explain our present. Rieff says modern people cannot abide the Buddhist notion that "clinging to the past, like clinging to the self, is a forlorn illusion." Yet "even constructed meanings are mortal," and eventually the past is lost: "death and forgetting are two sides of the same coin." For someone like me, who at times feels as though I am all history, the idea that I am fashioned out of dust is a jolting one.

What is the cost of holding to history? What is history anyway? Is history obscured by memory? And can memory be trusted? All these questions are posed by Rieff. Was the philosopher George Santayana right – are those who cannot remember the past condemned to repeat it? Rieff argues that we can make a fetish of the past, turning it into "a formula for unending grievance and vendetta." Far too often those who remember the past also repeat it, and memory hardens hatred:

> This is what happened in the American South after 1865 and, while diminished, is still happening today; it blighted the former Yugoslavia in the 1990s. Today it is endemic in Israel–Palestine, in Iraq and Syria, in the Hindu nationalist populism of India's Bharatiya Janata Party ... jihadis and Islamists ... Let there be no turning of a blind eye to the high price societies have paid and are continuing to pay for the solace of remembrance.

I have been guilty in the past of this blindness, and drawn to remembrance of suffering and trauma that can sustain victimhood. It is a response to a country that has written Indigenous people out of history, preferring instead what the anthropologist W.E.H. Stanner called the "Great Australian Silence." For many Indigenous people it is hard to move beyond grief when they are locked in a cycle of "sorry business"; a monotonous drumbeat of funeral marches. But remembrance doesn't necessarily stop the past repeating; sometimes it may even impede reconciliation and true justice. It is right to remember, but is it also right to forget?

The French historian Ernest Renan said, "Forgetting ... [is an] essential factor in the creation of a nation." This is what I meant to say in my speech: we are better than this. I spoke the truth of my family to rescue them from the Great Australian Silence – not to hold us there, but to liberate us from it. That so many have sought to break my words into pieces and deploy only those that best suit them speaks of the age of the politics of identity that too often shuts down debate and hardens division; this is identity too often unscrutinised and exclusive.

If the Australian Dream is rooted in racism, then it has been the struggle of Indigenous people to rise above it, even as the Australian nation has sought to atone for it. In acts of reconciliation, national apology, recognition of rights to land and native title, a willingness to review history; through marriage and friendship; in our High Court, our parliaments and our personal lives – in all of this, we are forging a nation. It is a project without end, as all nations are.

I want to look again at how, as individuals and communities, we are overcoming our past. I will trace the lives of our families and ancestors, who looked for ways to engage with Australia even when it told them they didn't belong. I want to challenge the politics of identity that can trap us in perpetual victimhood. I want to look at my life and the lives of many, many thousands of others who, like me, identify as Indigenous, and yet who – materially, socio-economically, romantically – are largely indistinguishable from – if not more privileged than – other Australians.

What emerges is, in many respects, a typical economic migration story. From the fringes of the frontier, Indigenous people started to connect with the colonial economy. Like migrants everywhere, they were marooned by the tides of history, the products of upheaval and violence, forced from their homes like refugees. Yes, there was exploitation – in parts of the country effectively a slave economy, a sorry history of stolen wages and unequal pay for an equal day's work. The legal battle continues for recompense. But whatever the circumstances, Aboriginal people were finding work on farms and fishing boats and cattle stations, in shearing sheds and on sugar plantations. This population was dynamic and mobile. They battled discriminatory and restrictive laws that governed the most private aspects of their lives and threatened the security of their families. These extraordinary people built communities, kept culture alive, befriended and married white Australians and served in this country's wars.

These Aboriginal pioneers, like migrants the world over, wanted a better life for their children. They measured their lives by their ability to provide for their children. Migrants look to what they have built, not what they have left behind, and so it has been for many Indigenous people. This is the story of my father, and his father and my great-great-grandfather, stretching back to well before Australia became a nation. They left a legacy of pride and would not countenance me shrinking from the challenges of life. I see their heirs everywhere in Indigenous communities. However hard it has sometimes been, and whatever grievances I still hold, becoming more engaged with mainstream Australia has made my life richer. Education and meaningful employment have allowed me to fulfil my dreams. With each step into a fascinating world, my horizons have broadened. Isn't this preferable to the fate of so many Indigenous people – indeed, members of my family and people I grew up with – who are destined for early graves? The Australian Dream works for most of us; isn't it time to ask if it can work for all of us?

We are bombarded with stories of dysfunction and disadvantage. The narrative is wedded to failure and deficit. It is a story plucked from the titles of books like Charles Rowley's *Outcasts in White Australia*, an outstanding piece of demographic research, which after its publication in the early 1970s significantly shaped our understanding of Indigenous communities. Many – black and white – voiced an identity based on rejection and exclusion. Yet *Outcasts* in fact charts the emergence of a new society, predominantly mixed-race, in which a people assumed to be dying out survive – frustrating and perplexing policy-makers – to find a place in Australia's suburbs and towns. Threaded through the pages of Rowley's seminal work is a story of Aboriginal agency – individuals striking out on their own or energising their communities, "the vast majority" of whom, he writes, "would have been looking to the settler economy for opportunity."

In a country where Indigenous fathers can be lampooned in mocking cartoons as delinquent dads; where government intervention and welfare control (arguably sometimes a useful palliative) risk removing the agency and responsibility of the people they are designed to assist, I hope this essay restores a belief that we are anything but hopeless and far from victims; that we can do it for ourselves because we have been doing it for ourselves. The sacrifice and resilience of our forebears has created a burgeoning Indigenous middle class: confident, self-assured. They are redefining what it is to be Indigenous, and expanding the idea of what it is to be an Australian in a multicultural country and a globalised world. The grandchildren of people who emerged from oppressive Aboriginal missions in a segregated Australia are as at home on the streets of New York as Dubbo.

There are those among us – black and white – who eschew economic development and social uplift as a new, disguised form of assimilation, preferring instead a story of failure and blame – as though culture and spirituality are antithetical to a modern globalised world. To their minds, success is not "black." I would say, tell that to my father: a Wiradjuri man, at various times a sawmiller, fruit picker, dam builder and tent boxer, who shed blood to feed his family and not take government handouts. Tell that to a man whose own father fought in a war for this country when his citizenship was denied, who came home to tell his son: no excuses. Tell that to a man who speaks his own language fluently, who has written the first Wiradjuri dictionary and helped rescue his traditions in order to teach a new generation. Tell him, because this is more his story than mine.

FINDING FRANK FOSTER

I have been trying to find Frank Foster for half my life. He has been the missing part of me. I have felt his presence like a phantom limb – an itch I cannot scratch. Frank Foster appears in my life so briefly and from a long time past, yet had he not existed I would not be who I am.

Until recently I knew little of this man who was my great-great-grandfather. Now Frank has spoken as if he were standing next to me. A chance conversation with a man whose family history wraps around mine has opened a window onto a past that illuminates so much of my present.

I was training at the gym at Redfern's National Centre for Indigenous Excellence. I go there not just for fitness, but to be with my people – to be renewed by community.

I began talking to a young man, Alan Daly, whom I see often. We usually nod and move on, but this day we stopped and over half an hour mapped our families. This is how we meet: Aboriginal people tracing our songlines, establishing our boundaries and confirming our identities.

Alan is from Sydney's La Perouse and I am from western New South Wales, but I told him of an old connection, a man named Frank Foster. Alan smiled and said, "I know him, I have something for you." Later that day he sent me a timeline, part of a community project to breathe life into people long gone, to sing the songs of ancestors. Here were the missing chapters of Frank's story.

Frank Foster emerges from the Australian frontier; his extraordinary and unusually long life (for Indigenous people of his era) spans a time when his people were forecast to die out, through to the birth of the new Australian nation, to the rise of the Aboriginal political voice in the 1930s. Grandfather Frank was born in 1870; his grandparents saw the coming of the whites. They were among the people of coastal Sydney, the clans of the Eora nation. They were those whom Captain Arthur Phillip – the governor of this new British penal colony – was instructed to protect and make friends with. After an initial period of curiosity and some amity, relations deteriorated and violence increased. The diaries of the marine officer Watkin Tench are a firsthand account of the early settlement. We see how soon British attitudes formed to the local people:

> That greater progress in attaching them to us has not been made I have only to regret ... to what cause then are we to attribute the distance which the accomplishment of it appears at? I answer to the fickle, jealous, wavering disposition of the people we have to deal with, who, like all savages, are either too indolent, too indifferent or too fearful to form an attachment ...

Within a matter of years Captain Arthur Phillip was ordering his soldiers to bring back the heads of black warriors he considered troublemakers.

By the time of Frank Foster's birth, his people had been ravaged by disease and settler violence. The settlement had expanded over the mountains to the west, where martial law had been declared against the Wiradjuri, as blacks and whites fought a long-running series of battles reported in the *Sydney Gazette* as an "exterminating war." Young Frank's life was about to take a dramatic turn that would see him forced from his homeland and merged with the remnants of the Wiradjuri people.

As the Aboriginal people were surrounded by death, their numbers decreasing, Sydney was booming. In the two decades from 1861 to 1881, the city's population grew from fewer than 60,000 to more than 220,000. This was a young metropolis, with its own theatres, newspapers, university, cathedrals, synagogue, town hall, banks and paved roads. The population explosion was the product of an economic expansion that for much of the nineteenth century would make the citizens of this collection of colonies the world's richest people.

Governor Lachlan Macquarie had lit the fuse with a public works program and by integrating former convicts and free settlers. He would also set a pattern for policy towards Indigenous people, elements of which continue to this day. Macquarie initially sought to extend kindness to the black population (however much kindness you could show to an invaded people). He held a feast day in Parramatta and encouraged them to engage with the local economy. There was much suspicion, with many Aboriginal people staying away for fear of having their children taken. Despite his assurances to the Aboriginal people, Macquarie was confronted with the task of managing an inevitable clash of cultures as the colony rapidly expanded. George Megalogenis in his book *Australia's Second Chance* – a chronicle of Australia's fluctuating economic fortunes – writes:

> The governor wanted to protect the children, especially in winter "when the weather is cold, the woods afford them little or no food, and they become prey to many loathsome diseases which poverty entails upon the human frame." He was aware that the "clearing of immense forests" for settler farming had deprived the locals of customary food sources – kangaroo, and more recently possum meat. From Macquarie's perspective, his was a policy of compassion, providing shelter and education. But from the Indigenous perspective it was the second act of dispossession. First the land had been taken, and now the white man wanted their children.

Macquarie's inclination to benevolence would be shattered by the 1816 Appin massacre in Sydney's southwest. Violence had broken out and the governor claimed he had to "protect the European inhabitants ... against these ... hostile and sanguinary attacks of the natives." He ordered the blacks cleared from the land. In his words he wanted to "strike terror" into the local Dharawal people, ordering his troops to force the locals to surrender as "prisoners of war," with those who were killed to be "hanged up on Trees in Conspicuous Situations." Aborigines were shot and beheaded, their skulls sent to England. On 17 April the soldiers struck, firing on a camp site; people fled, with some plunging over a cliff. Officially, fourteen people – among them women and children – were killed; Aboriginal people dispute that figure, claiming it was far higher. This year, on the 200th anniversary of the massacre, Dharawal descendant Gavin Andrews said he considered the attack a "declaration of war."

Macquarie set the template for the treatment of Aboriginal people. He oversaw forced child removal, accelerated the dispossession and escalated the violence. On his tomb is inscribed "the father of Australia" – for Aboriginal people, that is an epithet laced with hideous irony, but there is no doubt he set the economic and social direction of the young colony. As Megalogenis points out, he had drawn a line across the settlement "based on colour, not class." Former convicts were to have a place in this emerging nation, but Aboriginal inclusion would be conditional. Macquarie saw the future of the dispossessed first peoples – if they were to have a future – as contributing to his new economy. Megalogenis sums up: "the locals could only be accepted on the same terms as the migrants if they became like the migrants, agreeing to work for the greater good of the colony as farmers or servants." But was this possible?

W.E.H. Stanner, writing in the 1960s, believed that Aboriginal culture sat uncomfortably with Western notions of economy:

> The Dreaming and The Market are mutually exclusive. What is The Market? In its most general sense it is a variable locus in space and time at which values – the values of anything – are redetermined as human needs make themselves felt from time to time. The Dreaming is a set of doctrines about values – the value of everything – which were determined once for all in the past.

Stanner conceived of the Dreaming as a "heroic time of the indefinitely remote past." He coined the analogism "everywhen" – a place not fixed in time that "has for them an unchallengeable sacred authority."

Stanner explores this clash of cultures – between Dreaming and market – in his brilliant essay "Durmugam: A Nangiomeri." It traces Stanner's encounters with a man – Durmugam – from Daly River in the Northern Territory. The anthropologist meets the Nangiomeri "one wintry afternoon in 1932." Durmugam is painted with earth pigment and brandishing weapons for a large-scale fight. "The struggle could be seen to resolve itself into discontinuous phases of duels ... my eyes were drawn and held by an Aboriginal of striking physique and superb carriage." The Europeans called Durmugam "Smiler," an ironic nickname for a man widely feared and believed to be "the most murderous black in the region."

Stanner's essay spans fifty years of Durmugam's life and laments the decline of both the once-proud warrior and the traditions and beliefs that nurtured and sustained him. "The High Culture had not prospered; many of the young men openly derided the secret life." What Stanner observed was the transformation and decay that had begun after penetration of the region by foreigners in the 1870s. Aboriginal people had become "more familiar with Europeans and more dependent on their goods." He describes how the people began to "wander elsewhere to look for new goods and excitement." They developed a taste for European goods: tobacco, sugar, tea. Stanner describes their fascination with houses, vehicles and firearms.

The Nangiomeri were a people in transition, their numbers depleted, ravaged by disease, frontier violence and grog. The entire Aboriginal population was being remade. Stanner describes survivors regrouping, separate clans forming new affiliations, old borders dissolving: "Some of the small tribes ... had ceased to exist." What he describes are the fundamental push-and-pull factors of migration. Stanner himself uses that word to describe the upheaval. Migration is born of desperation and opportunity. Durmugam – like all migrants – seized the chance to reinvent himself: "A turning point came in his life when, in the middle of the 1920s, he met an energetic, vital European, who gave him work at a variety of jobs – mining, building construction, sleeper-cutting."

Migration and transformation are not without tension, or exploitation – and so it was for Durmugam and his people. They clung to traditional ceremony and custom even as they developed a parasitic dependence on the white economy.

> There was much disenchantment with Europeanism and constant friction with the farmers ... I found an unshaken belief that Aboriginal ways were right ... But the Aborigines were in chains: they could not

bear to be without the narcotic tobacco and the stimulating tea; any woman could be bought for a fingernail of one or a spoonful of the other.

Stanner was given to gloom about the fate of people like Durmugam. He feared for a society that had no real concept of a future, whose members were "as distant from the European as it was possible to be." The idea of the good life was now "inescapably connected to suffering." For Stanner, in the words of Robert Manne: "They were not merely a people without a concept of 'time' or 'history' but an 'ahistorical' people, a people without yearnings for the return of a Golden Age or the hope of salvation in the future ... for them, changelessness was both the desired and the anticipated state of the world."

Fellow anthropologist Gaynor Macdonald has challenged Stanner's assumptions. She has studied similar transitions among the NSW Wiradjuri people.

> Stanner underestimated the desire and ability of the Aboriginal people to change and develop because his own model blinded him to their creative efforts to encompass change. Had he desired, he would have been able to see these transformations around him in many parts of Australia, including New South Wales in the 1950s ... he was not looking for change.

Stanner equated change with an impertinent assimilation that assumed Aborigines would be subsumed into European life, losing all identity. He argued that assimilation should not be forced, that Aboriginal people should be able to choose their own destinies, embracing or rejecting white society as they saw fit. Stanner wanted appreciation of difference rather than the Great Australian Silence. But of course, Indigenous Australians are no more immune to the tides of history than anyone else: change was inevitable via government coercion; sheer weight of European numbers; economic dependence; the lure of materialism; temptation and curiosity, or just dogged survival. Stanner saw this himself, even if the full revelation eluded him.

Stanner encountered Durmugam again as a "white-haired" man of fifty-seven, with "failing eyesight, but still erect and still a tall striking figure of a man." The old warrior had lived in two worlds: old and new, black and white. The initiation-scarred, traditional lawman had also been the miner, builder and construction worker. His body was no longer painted with the earth, and the weapons of battle were laid down: "the blacks were on wages and very money-conscious; all had European clothes and in their camps ... one could find gramophones, torches, kitchenware, even bicycles; some of the younger people, though unable to read, were fond of looking at comic papers and illustrated magazines."

Stanner saw much sadness here. Rather than wonder at this synthesis and adaptation, he focused on what he perceived to be a loss of prestige and traditional authority. He was left with "the impression that the traditional culture was on its last legs." In Stanner's eyes Durmugam personified this decline. When Stanner last saw him, his family was in disarray, beset by abduction and sexual assault, with Durmugam humiliated after his favourite wife had run away with the son of his first wife. He told Stanner, "[I] would be better dead."

I share Gaynor Macdonald's view that Stanner can be guilty of seeing Aboriginal society as static and that (his empathy, humanity and intellect notwithstanding) he fails to appreciate our dynamism and individual agency. Stanner himself identifies the forces of migration among the local population, and for all migrants the journey is perilous and the outcome uncertain. No migrant emerges unchanged or unscathed. Durmugam's family travails and his people's precarious economic plight would not be unfamiliar to future waves of Greek, Italian, Lebanese, Vietnamese or Chinese immigrants to Australia. They too have faced culture shock, an assault on their traditions, a loss of authority and a communication breakdown with their uninterested children, who are estranged from their heritage.

I must confess to feeling uncomfortable with the migrant analogy even as I proffer it: how can I be a migrant in my own country? We did not seek a haven in this new country; it was often violently forced upon us. This nation's wealth was built on our land – land we were driven from. My migrant narrative does not negate the fact that the first peoples have rights inherent – rights still denied. But the hard fact of dispossession and the rapid growth of a world-leading economy, the imperative to prosper or perish, means I am the product of a great intracontinental black migration, and it starts with the man I began this story searching for: Frank Foster.

Grandfather Frank was a generation older than Durmugam. By the time he was born, the colony was approaching its centenary and Frank already bore a white man's name. In the 1870s, as the Europeans were just coming to Nangiomeri land, Frank Foster was a small boy living among the huddled remnants of the blacks of Sydney. He existed on rations and wrapped himself in blankets handed out to his people, who were believed doomed to extinction.

Frank and his family took shelter at Circular Quay. He lived with his father, also named Frank, and his mother, Elizabeth Matto, and two sisters, Bella and Bessie. The blacks had set up makeshift camps all around the Sydney shoreline, clinging to old tracks and places as a new city took shape around them. Frank was ten years old when his father died and the world he knew fell. Old Frank had been visiting a nearby Aboriginal camp and his death was recorded in the Sydney *Daily Telegraph* of 29 April 1880.

Reading that report today gives me a glimpse of a colony in transition: a Sydney where the black past was not yet pushed from sight, but rubbed embarrassingly against the genteel folk of a city that was already affecting airs and graces.

> For some weeks past a camp has been formed at Double Bay by a few
> of the aborigines who are wandering about Sydney. Yesterday one of
> the men inhabiting the camp, a half-caste named Frank Foster, died
> and as no doctor had attended him an inquest will be held upon the

remains today. The death was reported to the police, by whom the body was removed to the dead house, awaiting the inquest.

Three years later the Aborigines' Protection Board was established with the intention of controlling the lives of all Aboriginal people in New South Wales. It tallied the Aboriginal population in the state at 8919 and divided it into classifications of "full-blood" and "half-caste." The Board's report of 1883 makes it clear that the "half-castes" were to be integrated (albeit at a menial level) into the state's economy – continuing a fate pre-scribed by Lachlan Macquarie more than half a century earlier. The Protector, George Thornton, said:

> I maintain the opinion I have always held with regard to the half-caste portion of the aborigines viz, that they should be compelled to work in aid of their own requirements. They are well able to do so, having strength, experience and intelligence to qualify them for it; whilst I am of the opinion that the pure black should be taught, encouraged and aided in doing something for his own sustenance and comfort.

Thornton was frustrated, describing the "half-castes" as "indolent" and "useless," depriving the state of much-needed and scarce labour. He called for the establishment of reserves – in effect, migrant worker training camps – to enable them to "form homesteads, to cultivate grain, vegetables, fruit." Aborigines would become farmers. (As an aside, on 16 May 1892 the Board received an application from "William Grant, an Aboriginal" for a plot of land near Cowra: he was my paternal great-grandfather.)

The now fatherless Frank Foster and his mother and sisters were in the Protector's sights. The Board was tasked with clearing Sydney of blacks, whose camps Thornton considered an eyesore: "It cannot be fully described, except for language unfit for this paper ... as to the disgusting state of things among the aborigines ... at the government boatsheds at Circular Quay and Botany." Police reports reveal further the neglect and depravity. Sub-Inspector S.D. Johnson wrote of the Aborigines sheltered at Circular Quay:

> they have been a perfect nuisance, not only in this neighbourhood but also many of the public streets of the city, in consequence of their drunken and filthy habits. Several of them have been recently locked up during the night-time for drunkenness and filthy habits ... fighting and riotous behaviour.

The police reported begging, prostitution and violence among the "eighteen blacks huddled together in one sleeping place." Sub-Inspector John Donohoe was concerned that troops from British warships docked in the harbour might have to endure the scene, and suggested the blacks' "removal from the shed, more particularly as the Detached Squadron will be in port in a few days."

At the same time, the missionary Daniel Matthews had helped found a mission station at Maloga on the NSW–Victoria border. Matthews believed Christianity could protect the Aborigines from the racism of the frontier. Matthews was mocked for "having blacks on the brain": he believed Aborigines had been robbed of their birthright and encouraged the people to identify with the Jews by reading to them from the Old Testament. Matthews didn't know it, but he was stoking a fire that would give rise to the Aboriginal political movement. Among the people he took in was William Cooper, one of the most significant early political leaders. The historian Bain Atwood says:

> These narratives, as well as the sense of community Maloga encouraged, helped Aborigines formulate a sense of themselves as a race. More particularly, however, these histories enabled Aboriginal people to imagine themselves in terms akin to the persecuted and suffering Israelites ... they too had been dispossessed of their land.

Matthews was to have a significant bearing on Frank Foster's life after he and his family were rounded up from the Circular Quay boatshed and sent to the faraway Maloga mission.

Frank and his sisters were schooled by the missionaries. The records show he was a diligent and bright student. Extraordinarily, this boy hauled from the brutal camp at Circular Quay had ambitions to be a teacher. What's more, briefly he achieved this.

By 1889 Frank had left Maloga and, like so many other Aboriginal people, joined the great migration. He moved in search of work to the NSW south coast, which formed part of his ancestral homelands. He joined two other people, Hugh and Ellen Anderson, who had established a bark-hut school for Aboriginal kids in Kangaroo Valley. The NSW Department of Education sent an inspector to monitor Frank's progress. The government records describe Frank as "an intelligent half-caste." The inspector reported, "he reads and spells well and conducted a class in subtraction."

The school, however, was eventually closed and Frank was transferred to another mission, Warangesda, on the banks of the Murrumbidgee River at Darlington Point. At this new home he met a Wiradjuri girl named Lydia Naden and they had a daughter, Florence. I remember Florence as an old lady living on the mission in Griffith. We called her "Nanny Cot." She was my father's maternal grandmother: my great-grandmother. We would visit her each weekend. Her mind was slipping, the memories growing dim, but she would smile and touch our hands, connecting me to a timeless sense of belonging.

Florence lived her life without her father. Frank was banished from Warangesda for being impudent and refusing to obey the mission managers. He wanted to teach and the mission manager would not allow it. Frank moved through the missions, crisscrossing New South Wales and Victoria. The names – Cummeragunja, Warangesda – denote a shadow world where my people didn't die out but regrouped and formed new families that live on today.

From Warangesda, Frank Foster's tracks leave our family. I had known of him – just a name: the schoolteacher, they called him. But there was nothing to give flesh to this name. At each turn the traces of him became fainter. Until a fateful meeting at a gym in Redfern.

The Aboriginal people of La Perouse have put together their timeline, tracing the stories of ancestors like Grandfather Frank. Here were the missing chapters of Frank's story. It told how he wandered after Warangesda, moving from one community to another. He married several times and had more children; like so many other black men he found himself in jail, and spent his last years as a fisherman.

He lived on the NSW south-coast Aboriginal mission at Roseby Park and died in 1941. He is buried in the graveyard in the town of Berry. The funeral notice describes him as a "well known and respected identity ... and a great sufferer."

What a life he had led, what things he had seen. A boy of the brutal frontier who carried his swag through missions and dreamed of his books and his teaching. He was born into a people robbed of their land and he saw a new country – Australia – born, but was not counted among its citizens. He lost his home and looked for a new one. He loved and lost children. I hope he found peace – this great sufferer.

I will go to Berry soon and visit my old grandfather's grave. I have found Frank Foster.

Bill Stanner's memorable acquaintance Durmugam and my great-grandfather Frank lived a continent apart, but they were linked to the birth of Australia and its devastating impact on the first peoples. Theirs is a story of dispossession, forced removal, brutality and societal collapse. It is easy – and not entirely inaccurate – to see their lives as personal tragedies. This is a narrative we are familiar with. Stanner encouraged it with his insistence on an Aboriginal "everywhen" and a people caught between the Dreaming and the market, and a society locked in ancient and permanent traditions that would shatter at the touch of European modernity. Durmugam's journey from earth paint to collared shirt left him, in Stanner's telling, a broken man longing for death.

I could depict Grandfather Frank similarly, as a victim, a man of thwarted ambition, his liberty curtailed by the state, dying "a great sufferer." But I see something else, something Stanner observed but failed fully to appreciate. Frank and Durmugam's lives formed part of the great migration of Aboriginal people around the continent. These people were often forced off land; they were placed on reserves and trained as farmers and labourers; they travelled for work (Durmugam included); new kinships were formed, as disparate Aboriginal groups were bundled together, erasing ancient boundaries; later generations grew lighter, as many had children to the white newcomers. This was a nation forming: a people in transition, and governments – perplexed, frustrated, sometimes malignant – trying to manage it all.

Aboriginal people faced injustice and exploitation; families were shattered, sometimes irreparably so. Children were lost, their descendants vanishing into the new world with no trace of their Aboriginal origins. The suffering forms part of an intergenerational trauma that is at the root of so much contemporary misery. The inheritance of sadness informs much of Indigenous identity. But there is something else here, something that inspires me: these were people of resilience, pride, intelligence and dreams. In the twentieth century they would stand defiant against the state, demanding inclusion and equality; they would fight in foreign wars, send their kids to school, and lead another generation on the great migration for work, home and survival.

I thought picking grapes would be easy; I mean, how hard could it be? Outside, sunny day, wandering along the vineyards, plucking bunches and putting them in buckets. Just to sweeten the deal, I could eat them to my heart's content. And I was getting paid for this! Well, how wrong I was. I moved steadily along, row after row, mocking everyone else for being so slow. Then my mother – a demon worker – had to ruin it all.

"What about the grapes underneath?"

"Huh?"

Yes, under the vines: in the dirt was where I should go, back arched, neck bent, insects dive-bombing my eyes, with crushed grapes and warm, sticky grape juice running all over my face, my knuckles bleeding and scratched. That warm sunny day I was enjoying suddenly became a searing hell. This is how I learnt what work was, and it was a lesson in life: success doesn't come from the top of the vine; you have to get down in the dirt.

Each school holiday, my mother woke me early to take me with her and her sister to work as seasonal fruit pickers. We picked grapes, oranges and sometimes – worst of all – onions. For onions there was no shade of a vine, and rather than lying on my back looking up, I was standing: stooped, hamstrings burning, knees throbbing. My mother worked to supplement the money my father made from working for the local building supplier. I was being initiated into a time-honoured tradition for us blacks. It was what had brought us here. We were pickers: migrant workers.

My father always told me about what he called "the last walkabout." As a boy he lived with his family on the Aboriginal reserve at Condobolin in central-west New South Wales. These were the survivors of the frontier: the Wiradjuri people dispersed and scattered as settlers took up more and more of what was once our land. Some of the residents carried horrendous memories of violence. A local historian, Robert Ellis, wrote of an event that had become part of local folklore: the Mandagery Creek massacre. He learnt of it from old Jim Goolagong from the mission:

> The natives of the area were experiencing the kind of complete tribal breakdown which inevitably followed white settlement. One day the evident despair and distrust finally came to a head and the Aboriginal men, women and children began fighting among themselves. When the awesome battle came to an end almost every man, woman and child was either dead or dying. Some lay battered on the ground and others had actually climbed into the branches of high trees to die.

My father's father – like many Aboriginal men – enlisted in the army to fight in World War II. His older brother had died on the fields of France in World War I. My grandfather was already in his thirties, married with three young children and living in a country that didn't accord him full citizenship: he had many reasons not to go. But it was a critical decision that altered entirely the trajectory of his and his family's life, and set them on a course that eventually led to me in a new century returning to my grandfather's old Middle East battlegrounds, this time as a journalist reporting my own generation's wars.

My grandfather returned from the war determined he would get his family off the mission and out of the control of the state and welfare authorities. The Murrumbidgee Irrigation Area had started thirty years earlier and the region was rich in orchards and farms promising work; my grandfather decided that was the place for him. My father says many of the black families on the Condobolin mission loaded what they could onto horses and carts and set out on their long walk: it was around 300 kilometres from Condobolin to Griffith.

This trek is detailed in the book *Survival Legacies* by the architect Peter Kabaila. He maps the missions and settlements of New South Wales, tracking the movement of people. His book is rich in oral histories and reminiscences. It challenges what he says is "the continuous and persistent romanticisation of Aborigines by white people, [while] Aborigines became urban people." We became urban by moving. *Survival Legacies* is an intimate account of a mass migration:

> In the 1940s some people on large pastoral stations found work shearing, droving, crutching, boundary riding, fencing and clearing ... Aboriginal families provided labour for the Murrumbidgee Irrigation Area at the new irrigation towns of Griffith and Leeton, where there was both fruit picking and cannery work.

My father's family and the others who set out from Condobolin mission settled outside Griffith in a camp they dubbed "Condo Lane." Griffith was a magnet for Aboriginal people from across the state and even Victoria. A new reserve was set up at the intersection of three bridges on the edge of town; we called it the Three Way mission. The Three Way was in a very real sense a migrant workers' camp. Long-time resident Gloria Goolagong told Kabaila: "There were also people who came to the 'Three Way' just to do the fruit picking. They would take over any hut that wasn't vacated. We didn't have a lot of prize possessions at that time – mainly blankets and clothes – so moving was easy."

What was happening in Griffith was happening elsewhere. In fact, contrary to the popular story of resistance, violence and segregation (albeit a common pattern) there was an alternative and long history of economic accommodation. The anthropologist Ian Keen edited a study, *Indigenous Participation in Australian Economies*, that counters "the relative invisibility of Aboriginal people ... in economic histories." Aboriginal people could be both segregated and needed. The economist Christopher Lloyd lays bare this colonial contradiction: "Indigenous people developed economic relations with settlers in some places and supplied some labour while at the same time being marginalised and impoverished due to land seizures."

The settler economy grew out of the land grabs of the nineteenth century, sparking "mutual dislike, distrust and open hostility." Despite that contentious relationship, a hybrid economy took shape.

The traditional lands had been penetrated and [Aboriginal people] were now in a partially dependent relationship. On the other hand the emerging settler-capitalist forms on the frontier also had to adapt, and that meant sometimes using Indigenous people as labourers, trading with Indigenous people for food supplies and using traditional knowledge.

In the early decades of the nineteenth century, relations between white and black were being recast across the colony. The anthropologist John White shows how on the NSW south coast in the decade after first contact in the 1830s, local Aborigines and settlers formed reciprocal relationships. Aboriginal people even guided the newcomers to the land with "good grass and water." The settlers were at times saved from starvation by Aborigines providing food: fish and oysters. They rescued survivors of wrecked ships.

The pastoral and cattle industries were well suited to this form of economic adaptation. Aboriginal people could work seasonally or intermittently, live on ancestral land and maintain aspects of traditional culture. Farmers and station owners, in return, gained a stable supply of cheap and – often – exploitable labour. It was not exactly a win-win – the power balance was strongly in the settlers' favour – but Aboriginal people were using and selling their knowledge and capacity as they adapted and survived.

Such employment ebbed and flowed with the economy and changes to restrictive laws. But Aboriginal people filled the breach during the labour shortage of World War II. Aboriginal unemployment in the Murrumbidgee region fell from more than 30 per cent to as little as 4 per cent at this time. Like my family, these people were crop pickers.

The post-war Aboriginal migration and economic integration (admittedly often forced and far from egalitarian) occurred amid great social, economic and demographic change in Australia. Arthur Calwell, immigration minister and future Labor leader, described it as a critical time, giving the country twenty-five years to "make the best possible use of our second chance to survive." Australia's ageing population meant it needed more people, and with the White Australia policy limiting options, the government looked to Europe. The then Opposition leader and later prime minister Robert Menzies, countering opposition to large-scale immigration, said: "If we wait for economic perfection before building up our population, we shall someday find that our lack of population has invited an attack from which our entire economy will be destroyed. Every one of us in this country is either a migrant or a descendant of one."

Menzies wasn't including Indigenous people in that, but he could have. We were mostly the descendants of immigrants too. By the post-war era, many people identifying as Aboriginal had mixed heritage: for me, Irish convict stock and a white grandmother of English/German background. Charles Rowley points out that the number of so-called "half-castes" rivalled, and in some parts of the country surpassed, the number of "full-bloods." Within a generation, in what was known as the "settled areas," a majority of Indigenous people were of mixed origin.

In Queensland, for example, Rowley says, the most reliable count "indicated that half-castes outnumbered Aboriginals ... by approximately 11,000 to 8,000." This was radically altering not just physical appearance but the whole nature of the Aboriginal society, and in turn the overall make-up of the nation. Rowley says by 1961, "the part-Aborigines were one of the most rapidly increasing groups of people anywhere in the world and Aborigines of the full descent were also increasing much more rapidly than the non-Aboriginal population, exclusive of the effects of migration."

No wonder they wanted more Italians and Germans! Seriously, though, this black population boom created some fear (it was thought white Australia might be overrun!) and much exasperation and bewilderment. Colour mattered; Australia was obsessed with it. Governments and administrators tied themselves in knots trying to define who was and was not Aboriginal. Courts could decide on sight to which category an individual belonged. Aboriginal people could be moved in and out of columns: people judged to be three-quarters Aboriginal were often counted with full-bloods; half-castes associating with those deemed "Aboriginal" received a different classification to those living separately; children born of two half-castes had a separate category; families were segregated, with some individuals exempt from restrictive laws – dog-tags, as they were colloquially known. All of this amounted to state-run experiments in social engineering.

The experiment had a name: assimilation. It was a policy born out of the initial conference of the Commonwealth and State Aboriginal Authorities in Canberra in 1937. The stakeholders came together to solve this "half-caste problem." It was a time when officials openly talked of the evil half-caste, the offspring of "low white men" and black women. Some suggested sterilisation as an answer. It was widely assumed that these mixed-race children inherited the worst of both races and were beyond redemption. Others argued that there might be enough of the "superior" white blood in them to allow them to pass into the general population. What really horrified them – and here they were talking about my family – was half-castes marrying half-castes and creating a whole new population potentially beyond state control.

A.O. Neville and J.W. Bleakley were big figures at the conference as Protectors of Aborigines in Western Australia and Queensland respectively. Both were seized by their mission to control the breeding of "half-castes." There were laws regulating marriage and in parts of the country it was an offence for white men to have sex with Aboriginal women. Writing in 1929, Bleakley said, "the cross-breed element provides the most difficult part of the 'Aboriginal' problem." Later in life, he reflected that "all mixed-blood races labour under social and temperamental handicaps." He said the problem was "Aboriginal temperament"; even being raised by whites made little difference because it was "not so much a matter of the colour of the skin as the colour of the mind."

Bleakley favoured segregation and carefully managing who was capable of joining white society. He preferred half-castes to marry each other, so as to maintain a separate distinct population. A.O. Neville, too, monitored and controlled marriage and breeding, but believed that "ultimately the natives must be absorbed into the white population of Australia." Writing later, Rowley regards Bleakley and Neville as "kindly and well meaning" but labouring under "common racist assumptions of the Australian folklore." The 1937 conference set a new policy paradigm and resolved that, "The destiny of the natives of aboriginal origin, but not of the full blood, lies in their ultimate absorption by the people of the Commonwealth and it is therefore recommended that all efforts be directed to that end."

How would the "half-castes" be absorbed? Like migrants, through the economy. It is clear that administrators saw the need to train the growing mixed population for work. Rowley points out that the conference delegates believed that "if detribalised, they should be employed and educated." A.O. Neville said, "they must be taught to read and write and count, know what wages they could get, make arrangements with employers." During the war years, Aboriginal people, usually exploited as cheap labour, could get full award wages. M.T. McLean, the Chief Protector for South Australia, explicitly made the link with migration, saying the answer was absorption, "as with the Greek and Italian migrants."

The 1937 conference set a course for my family as decisively and surely as did European settlement and dispossession 150 years earlier. Policy, though, is only half the story; how did Aboriginal people respond to it? If colour mattered to whites, then it mattered to blacks too. Some light-skinned Aboriginal people were counted as Australians in the census, while their darker relatives were excluded. Some half-castes could be exempted from restrictive laws and segregation – an honorary white citizenship. In parts of the country those deemed "quarter-caste" were considered "white."

Anthropologists identified a hierarchy of colour. In Victoria, as far back as the late 1800s, light-skinned people were being removed from missions to fend for themselves in the broader economy. Rowley points out that a two-tiered Aboriginal society was developing. When it came to "absorption," some were clearly more favoured – and "in practice it tends to be the part-aboriginal family of light caste which is selected to move into a house in town."

This was a critical era. Some were leaving the missions, while those more obviously "Aboriginal" were left behind. (The fault-line is still obvious today.) Aboriginal people themselves were redefining their identities. Charles Rowley reproduced this letter from a "part-Aboriginal" woman in Western Australia:

> they want to pass a law to say we half-castes, whether we are 90 per cent white blood ... living in a position as good as many white people, are still aborigines, and are still on the same footing as those on the fringe of civilisation. If we are law abiding and are getting an honest living, are we not British subjects? I think we are entitled to citizenship.

The anthropologist Ruth Fink surveyed the people of one western NSW town and found that among twenty-five Aboriginal families who considered themselves superior to other blacks, in almost half the cases their claim to status was based on being married to a white person.

Peter Kabaila in *Survival Legacies* notes this shift in identity. He says this new generation of Aborigines of mixed descent "began to taste the white man's life, and decided by comparison, Aboriginal lives were poor." Assimilation today is a dirty word and for good reason, but it opened a door to Australia, and unlocked opportunity and potential. Speaking to Kabaila, Eddie Kneebone, a Pangerang man, says assimilation is just a word; the reality is undeniable:

> we are descended from the traditional people, into what we call urban Aboriginals. Whether we like it or not, we use cars, we spend money, we dress ourselves, we work in a white man's job from nine-to-five. If I use the word assimilation, it is the truth, whether you like it or not.

The assimilation era was a strange time. The government was trying to cleanse the Aboriginal population – wash them into white Australia while condemning those thought "unacceptable" to rot on repressive, restrictive missions and settlements. The "respectable blacks" boasted of keeping their houses spotlessly clean, wore collars and ties and went to church on Sunday. But old racism died hard, and they still faced small-town segregation; if they went to the cinema, they would have to sit in roped-off sections and were often barred from local pubs and swimming pools.

Were some Aboriginal people suffering from a "Stockholm syndrome" – the captive loving their captor? Yes, but don't imagine all were supplicants: far from it. These were people with determination, intellect and resilience, expressing their own free will and aspiring to realise their dreams. Indigenous leaders were making their voices heard. William Cooper in the 1930s started the Australian Aborigines' League; the league's secretary was Doug Nicholls, a star footballer and later governor of South Australia. Cooper, like Nicholls, was a devout Christian, raised on the same missions on the Murray River as my great-great-grandfather Frank Foster. He petitioned King George, calling for His Majesty's intervention to "prevent the extinction of the Aboriginal race," improve conditions and support Aboriginal members of parliament. In Sydney on Australia Day 1938, Cooper joined other Aboriginal political leaders in the Day of Mourning.

Cooper and others were exploring the limits of his people's rights and their place in Australia. He even suggested the formation of an Aboriginal state, an idea that is still being advocated today by Indigenous leaders such as lawyer Michael Mansell. Cooper saw land as central, not only as a matter of justice but also as a way of building an economic base. He called for land to be returned for farming, education and technical training. He argued for fair wages and pensions on the same basis as white Australians. Intriguingly, Cooper too linked the struggle of the Aboriginal economic migrants to the influx of new European immigrants. It is a recurring theme, as the various categories of Aborigines struggled to define what this assimilated Australia would mean for them.

My paternal grandfather, Cecil Grant, was born in the first decade of the twentieth century onto the fringes of the frontier. His life embodies the shift of Aboriginal people from outcasts to Australians. He was at times a shearer, rodeo bull-rider, rabbit-trapper, fruit picker and soldier: his personal journey in the great black migration from mission to town was a distance of mere miles, but an epochal trek. He was a friend of Doug Nicholls and of another seminal Aboriginal leader, Bill Ferguson, and campaigned with them for citizenship and rights. In 1966 – a year before the most successful referendum in Australia's history decided that Aboriginal people would be fully counted in the national census – he stood for election as the Aboriginal representative on the Aborigines Welfare Board, a body that exercised an often fearsome control over black lives.

I found my grandfather's campaign pitch, along with those of the other candidates, in an edition of the Aboriginal Welfare Board's newsletter, *Dawn*, a magazine distributed to Aboriginal people throughout New South Wales. It is an extraordinary time capsule where we hear the voices of people and the quaint, paternalistic tone of officials, whose echo can still be heard in our era of "closing the gap." Writing in the November/December 1966 issue, E.A. Willis, the board's chief secretary, says:

> There is still much that needs to be done, but the tide has turned – we are now moving more quickly toward social and economic equality.
>
> We have no magic wand to give us unlimited finance or to repair the accumulated defects of nearly two centuries, but the nearest thing to such a wand is the mutual self-help and cooperation of the Aboriginal people.

Fifty years later we hear an echo in Prime Minister Malcolm Turnbull's pledge to "speak with and not to Indigenous people" (and when I interviewed him in 2016, he substituted "no magic bullet" for E.A. Willis's "no magic wand").

The campaign platforms of my grandfather's fellow candidates make for revealing reading. Most of them speak of their Christianity, and economic empowerment; they call for "fishing and economic cooperatives"; for Aboriginal reserves to be turned into farms: "if we can work farms for white men we can do it for ourselves"; they talk of their people needing to "shoulder responsibility" for their plight (again finding its echo today). All of the men stressed their work ethic and desire to find a place in modern Australia. As one said, "I have held numerous jobs from farm hand, fisherman, mill hand, factory worker, sewerage ganger, miner, etc; to my present position and according to all reports I am accepted everywhere."

My grandfather spoke of his people's inherent, God-given equality:

> I've heard the Aborigines question discussed at various levels – from the man-in-the-street, to shearing sheds, in Army camps and at meetings of the Federal Advancement for Aborigines Organisation. To me, they present one fact and that is that anyone claiming that Aborigines are not humanly equal to other people seems to lack knowledge of the common ingredients of which all human beings are made ... we are humanly equal and should be regarded by all as such ...

These are the powerful voices of the Aboriginal economic migration. They emerged from the missions, lives bound and controlled, to demand a seat at the table. They are people with a straight-backed dignity, resolute in the demand for their rights. I am drawn to photographs of the people of this era. They are immaculate: suits and ties, pork-pie hats. My grandfather had a daily ritual: home from work, a bath, and a crisp white shirt – never to be seen in town in anything less. William Cooper, with his shock of grey hair perfectly swept back and an extravagant moustache, looks like an English lord or a commanding general of the American Civil War. A generation earlier, their fathers were hunted down, rounded up and put in chains.

I am in awe of these people. To imagine them now as victims defames their memory. Assimilation was a policy predicated on the "evil of the half-caste"; a problem to be solved; a people to be "absorbed." It was about burying your mother – abandoning your culture in shame. That was the intention, but the people of my grandfather's generation also saw an open door and marched through it. They didn't appeal for equality; they assumed it. When I look at them, I see individuals exercising choice, shaped by their world as they in turn shaped it. Some passed as white people, crossing the street to avoid dark relatives lest their secret be exposed; others held tight to their communities. All were alive to the possibilities of life in a booming Australia. They looked at the post-war migration and hitched a ride, becoming economic migrants themselves. The meagre pay and menial work didn't dissuade them, as they – admittedly often in desperation – fought to provide for their families.

Character, ethics, honour and courage: these are the things of eternity. These virtues transcend race and speak to us all – challenge us all. Aristotle spoke of these things. In *The Nicomachean Ethics*, he said virtue was a choice as surely as vice: "Saying 'No' is up to us, so is saying 'Yes' ... acting, when it is noble, is up to us; not acting, when it is shameful, is also up to us." These Aboriginal heroes were saying yes, striking out in a country that had rejected them.

This was a complex world with its own contradictions, and among Aboriginal people, as in all communities, there were winners and losers. Assimilation solidified a hierarchy of colour that was already evident. The seeds were being sown for class divisions that would dramatically widen. Lighter skin, marriage to a white person, a house up-town, regular employment, kids in school – all of this would alter an Aboriginal society that previously was bound to a shared fate. The risk-takers, the mobile, the self-motivated were rewarded, while another population remained behind, their lives growing harder and more impoverished.

A decade ago the late academic Maria Lane observed these two diverging Indigenous populations. An Aboriginal woman, Lane saw the emergence of a fledgling "Open Society" – opportunity-, effort- and outcome-oriented – by contrast with an "Embedded Society" – risk-averse, welfare- and security-oriented. The two populations, she said, "are linked through kinship and continuing interaction," but their courses were set by the great Aboriginal migration. Lane called it the "slow grind," creating a new paradigm founded on "universal human rights, the rights to a rigorous, standard education and equal rights to a place in the Australian society and economy – recognizably a much more liberal, even bourgeois ideology, individualist and competitive."

These were the people on the move from the 1940s to the 1970s; leaving settlements and missions and throwing off the heavy hand of government control. They are journeys I have already traced through my family, but the timing was crucial, their movement coinciding with periods of economic growth and increased opportunity. As Lane said, "it was a risky move into the unknown, but one that for most paid off," just as it did for other economic migrants drawn from the far-flung corners of the earth.

> The comparison with the experience of migrant groups is inescapable: although migrants from Greece and Italy and Yugoslavia and Lebanon in the fifties and sixties were expected to be content with employment on factories and on farms, they also did not expect their children to follow them: very often, in the second generation, their children have gone straight into tertiary education and professional employment. I am suggesting that a high proportion of Indigenous people have followed a similar path.

When Lane picked up their story, the grandchildren and great-grandchildren of these pioneers were emerging into higher education. She focused on South Australia and found that in less than a decade, from the late 1990s to the mid-2000s, the number of Indigenous students entering the last year of high school doubled, and the number gaining good university entrance scores had likely tripled. These young, smart achievers were part of a population boom. Their parents were more often black and white, as rates of intermarriage increased. Put simply, these kids were of two worlds and redefining what that meant for them.

At the same time there was a parallel Aboriginal universe: a shadow world of choking poverty, rivers of grog, frightening rates of violence, over-crowded housing and intergenerational unemployment. While the children of Lane's Open Society were graduating high school, their Embedded Society cousins were committing suicide at rates ten times that of the rest of the Australian population, or were graduating from juvenile detention to adult prison. This is the Indigenous society so maddeningly familiar to Australians, the lost lives in too many news and current affairs stories.

The Embedded Society were those left behind. Maria Lane mapped their journey too. Many never left the settlements of the segregation era; others ventured to small towns and stayed. Some returned to the old familiar places or eventually made their way to the city. Crucially, and tragically, most found themselves on the wrong side of history, moving in economic downturns – when jobs were scarce and the open world less welcoming. These people became locked in cycles of welfare dependency and social decay at a time when government policy – however well inten-tioned – made "sitting down" easier. They became embedded.

No broad social sketch can be complete or entirely accurate: individuals are too unpredictable and there is the risk of falling into caricature and stereotype. A great sense of community and enduring family bonds are to be found in the Embedded Society. Even amid dysfunction and disadvan-tage there can be a comforting sense of belonging. I know them – they are family – and they are generous and loving and loyal. Life in the Open Society can be lonely and alienating, and even the most successful Indigenous people are not immune from random and hurtful racism. It is wrong to ascribe too much of the fate of these two populations to the vagaries of personal choice or questions of character. Like all of us, they are products of history, economy, timing and luck – decisive factors often beyond their control. Yet Lane identified a schism in the black population, puncturing the lazy assumptions and convenient identity of a homo-genous, united Indigenous society: no, we are not all the same.

THE IDENTITY TRAP

> "What do I have in common with the Jews? I hardly have anything
> in common with myself."
>
> — Franz Kafka

Zimbabwe is a strange place in which to feel liberated. Life under Robert Mugabe is not something I would willingly choose. But this was the first place I touched down outside Australia. I was en route to South Africa to cover the end of apartheid. I waited, in a swelteringly hot airport lounge drinking warm Coca-Cola, for a connecting flight to Johannesburg and no one knew or cared that I was Aboriginal. I was a world away from the history that had shaped me. I was free from having to explain myself or conform to a particular identity. These people were black in ways that I wasn't. They were Africans, and to them I was simply an Australian.

The idea that I am Australian hits me with a thud. It is a blinding self-realisation that collides with the comfortable notion of who I am. To be honest, for an Indigenous person, it can feel like a betrayal somehow – at the very least, a capitulation. We are so used to telling ourselves that Australia is a white country: am I now white? That I am an Indigenous person is a fact of birth: my father is a Wiradjuri man from central and southwest New South Wales; my mother is from the Kamilaroi people of the state's north-west. That is who I am but not all I am. The reality is more ambiguous, defying easy definition even as I may prefer to cloak it in a veil of certainty. To borrow from Franz Kafka, identity is a cage in search of a bird.

I was born into the "half-caste" community that emerged from the Australian frontier; this hybrid society formed out of the clash of the first peoples and the new. They married each other and repopulated in harsh segregated missions and settlements designed to Christianise and "civilise" us as the pillow was being smoothed for the slow death of a people. Being an "outsider," something other, sits more simply with our history of exclusion and injustice. And my family has suffered, through generations lived at the coalface of poverty and bigotry. I was born into a life on the margins, as I have written in *Talking to My Country*: "We lived in Australia and Australia was for other people."

But I have grown from the boy I was and my country has grown from the land it was. Can I truly see privilege as "white"? Is it "black" to suffer crippling disadvantage? If these things are true, then I am assuredly "white." I am an Australian, with all the privilege that brings. I am in the highest-earning category in the country, I live in a nice house, I have a good car, I can eat out and not bother to check the bill; my children have been to the best schools money can buy, not just in Australia but around the world. I have had a career that has allowed me to realise all my dreams.

"Australians all, let us rejoice!" I have a lot to rejoice about.

Am I a "coconut"? That is the put-down Indigenous people use for those suspected of trying to "pass." It means being brown on the outside and white on the inside. It is meant to hurt, but it says more about the person levelling the taunt than the intended victim. It is the insult of the weak: people whose own identity is fraught and fragile. That isn't surprising: Aboriginal people have historically been defined and redefined in and out of existence. The Australian Law Reform Commission counts since settlement sixty-four separate categories of "Aboriginal": a Heinz soup range of blackness. The academic Marcia Langton summed up this Indigenous predicament in her book *Well, I Heard It on the Radio and I Saw It on the Television*: "For Aboriginal people, resolving who is Aboriginal and who is not is an uneasy issue, located somewhere between the individual and the state."

I saw the painful truth of this only recently when an Aboriginal man – whom I will call Keith – asked me to help verify his identity. This man had lived his life as an Aboriginal person, born into a small, tight-knit rural community. Keith was taken from his family as a boy and raised in state-run welfare homes. He has struggled with periods of homelessness and unemployment, has lost a child to a drug overdose and is now raising his granddaughter in inner-city government housing, surrounded by noise and violence. Keith applied to move, but was required to show proof of Aboriginality. He approached the local land council, who refused him on the basis that he was not a council member.

Keith is a victim of the Commonwealth legal definition of Aboriginality. It is a three-pronged process built around ancestry, self-identification and community acceptance. To "qualify" as an Aboriginal person, one must get the endorsement of an Indigenous organisation: a letter of Aboriginality. I cannot think of a more degrading, demoralising and potentially devastating process. I have never sought, nor would I ever seek, any such proof of who I am. But Indigenous people are constantly reminded that their identities are in question – reminded of the box they must belong to. It is there in every official form – when we enrol our children in school, join a sporting organisation, apply for a loan or fill in the national census, the box demands to be ticked: are you Aboriginal or Torres Strait Islander? No one else in Australia is asked to define themselves so exclusively.

Marcia Langton, herself an accomplished Indigenous woman, has cautioned against a creeping sense of Indigenous exceptionalism – a belief in entitlement – tied to identity, which can deter Aboriginal and Torres Strait Islander people from joining the mainstream of Australian life.

Aboriginal people are bound to a communal identity. This can impose a rigid conformity, accompanied sometimes by an intimidating lateral violence. Self-righteous Indigenous people take on the role of "identity police," deciding who is in or out. All the while, Aboriginal people face having to explain themselves to a wary, sceptical, ignorant – even hostile – Australian public.

There is vigorous debate within the Indigenous community that bristles against a narrowly defined identity. It can feel like a straitjacket. Yin Paradies is an example of someone with Indigenous heritage who chafes at orthodox interpretations of identity. An academic of Indigenous–Anglo-Asian heritage, Paradies says he represents both "coloniser and colonised," "black and consummately white." He has described a "prison-house of identity" that means his efforts to express a hybrid sense of himself lead to attacks on his authenticity. He says he has been called a "coconut" and a "nine-to-five black" taking a job from a "real Aborigine."

Paradies is typical of many urban Indigenous people in having a circle of friends who are non-Indigenous, and in having little contact with extended family. He doesn't deny that Aboriginal people have suffered "a deplorable history of marginalization, discrimination and exclusion," but that doesn't solely define him. Yet, he says, Aboriginal people looking to history for their identity have no trouble finding white supporters to encourage them, and to accord them an unquestioned expertise. Being Aboriginal can be a qualification in itself:

> The idea that indigeneity is synonymous with suffering and marginality, together with the misconception that such "victimhood" bestows privileged access to social truths, leads to uncritical acceptance of the views, opinions and scholarship of Indigenous people about Indigenous issues.

A former public servant, Kerryn Pholi, publicly renounced her "Aboriginal identity" in an article she titled "Why I burned my 'Proof of Aboriginality'". She said she grew tired of being a "professional Aborigine" in the "Aboriginal industry." Pholi said that, like others, she worked in Aboriginal-identified positions and would "harangue a room full of people with real qualifications and decades of experience with whatever self-serving, uninformed drivel ... happened to pop into my head." She said there was "nothing special" in being able to trace her ancestry back to a "stone-age way of life." She was "grateful to the 'white invaders'" for lifting her into modernity. Pholi said she didn't feel "particularly proud to be Aboriginal," which she equated with a "skinhead thumping his chest and saying he is proud to be white." What pride she did feel, she wrote, came from the fact that "at some point my Aboriginal ancestors had the wit to take advantage of what was on offer."

I quote Pholi merely to illustrate the bind a rigid concept of Aboriginal identity can place us in. Pholi rejects her Aboriginality with the same zealotry as those who proselytise the moral superiority of Indigenous people. She lacks the subtlety and nuance of Yin Paradies' writings. Where he seeks to illuminate and broaden the discussion of the possibilities of multilayered identity, Pholi ridicules the notion of any unique Indigenous worldview. Her focus on being a "professional Aborigine" is appropriate, because she writes like a disgruntled employee who has slammed the door on the way out and is now furiously tweeting insults about her former colleagues. But despite Pholi's intemperate and tabloid language, her article is not entirely bereft of insight. Indigenous identity has been corporatised and exploited for profit by some Aboriginal and non-Aboriginal people.

The political scientist Terry Moore offers a more penetrating analysis, focusing on how government has adopted contemporary notions of Aboriginal identity which elevate the importance of difference and resistance, thereby denying Aboriginal people the "potential of being both Aboriginal and Australian, being different and belonging. They maintain Aboriginal marginality." Moore writes of a "mythological Aboriginality" that does not reflect the lived reality of many Indigenous people. Aboriginal urban elites and their supporters, Moore says, perpetuate this while simultaneously stigmatising whiteness. In short: rejecting whiteness makes you more black.

At various stages of my life, I have probably been as guilty as anyone of assuming superiority and enhancing difference that can lead to divisiveness. I caught a glimpse of my younger, naive self when a group of young people took to the stage at a conference of Indigenous people in Victoria. They were impressive: confident and articulate, but with all the foolishness of youth. One of them, an especially vocal young woman with a permanent earnest frown and obviously of mixed heritage, spoke of wanting to "dismantle her whiteness" and the need to "rid education of whiteness." I allowed myself a wry grin and a shake of the head, thinking, well, there goes Shakespeare, Einstein and Newton; I wondered from where she would derive her politics without Marx or her philosophy without Foucault! She said she was tired — an amusing thought: tired at twenty-five! — of constantly explaining herself to white people, and now associated only with other black people. This was precisely what Terry Moore warned about: anti-white superiority.

The girl was obviously a thinker and a reader and feeling her way in the world; she thought herself a radical but was in fact a reactionary, and will hopefully grow up and out of her ideas. But harmlessly amusing as she was, the ideas are dangerous. We live in a world and an era of sharp identity politics that is wreaking devastation. Look around: the resurgence of political populism on the left and right; hardening and violent sectarian divisions; hyper gender and racial awareness and division; a stultifying climate of debate where the participants lecture, abuse and try to silence rather than discuss and reason. There is an absence of manners and generosity and a loss of perspective. Politicians argue that "people have a right to be bigots," and media commentators with the loudest megaphones in the land complain about an attack on their free speech.

We walk a precipice when we analyse identity: Indigenous identity, especially. I am sensitive to those who have suffered terribly for identity denied or imposed. Aboriginal skulls rest in glass jars, hostages to the long-abandoned pseudo-sciences of phrenology and eugenics that judged my ancestors a lower form of humanity. Simply to survive here we had to overcome those who would breed us out. Children were separated from families and instructed to "act white, think white, be white." Poking and prodding identity only risks reopening old wounds. I am cautious, too, lest my words be twisted and taken up by arch-assimilationists, who would prefer we abandon all allegiance to family and heritage to become — what they benignly refer to as — just Australians: an identity that they reserve the right to define and confer.

Trepidation aside, I should not be deterred from examining identity, particularly my own. Whatever my questions, I have a deep attachment to those I see as "my people": a fraternity akin to that felt by Jewish people, wherever in the world they come from and despite their differences. I share a common history, a kinship, elements of culture and a concern for the future with other people who similarly identify broadly with being Indigenous. With just a passing nod in the street, we can tell each other we are still here. We understand each other in a way that sometimes still eludes me even with those non-Indigenous people closest to me. There is no one I could love more than my wife, yet there are times when we could be speaking different languages: mine from my Aboriginal roots and hers as a white Australian. Rather than separating us, I see our differences as the grit that polishes our relationship.

Identity is a two-way mirror – what we project and what others perceive. As the broader Australian community has constructed its image of what an Indigenous person is, so we conform to meet expectations. There are those whose physical appearance leaves no doubt about their heritage; the state endorses Aboriginality by acknowledgment of native title claims or land rights; there are others who need to resort to what the historian Tony Judt called "the comfort of received wisdom" – in our case a reliance on a narrative of historical grievance and exclusion and an attachment to cultural markers or artefacts.

Precarious Aboriginal identity has been buttressed by a sense of pan-Indigenous unity built around shared injustice, experience of contemporary racism, revival of "culture" (often reimagined), supposedly innate spirituality and, often, rejection of whiteness. Bronwyn Carlson in *The Politics of Identity* places history at the centre of identity: "This history is vast and varies across the country and across time periods, encompassing Aboriginal experience from pre-colonial to colonial and subsequent periods. It is represented in the oral or recorded memories of Aboriginal people ... this history is not past or done with."

But history is passed on as memory: selective and infused with imagination. The French historian Jacques Le Goff warns that "memory only seeks to rescue the past in order to serve the present and the future."

Our world is awash with the politics of memory. The Chinese remind themselves of the "hundred years of humiliation by foreign powers"; Vladimir Putin speaks of the "tragedy" of the collapse of the Soviet Union; the Jewish people pledge to "never forget" the Holocaust; the Palestinians remember the Nakba, the "catastrophe" of the establishment of the state of Israel; Donald Trump pledges to "make America great again." Of course the motives vary and some claims have greater virtue, but history and memory can be potent weapons in constructing identity. Memory − history − can embolden a sense of victimhood, a superiority of suffering.

History, suffering and culture can each encourage a narrowly conceived, "essentialist" identity. There is a performative aspect to this: adopting a manner of speech as "Aboriginal English," inventing or reclaiming traditional-sounding names, or physically cloaking oneself in "Aboriginality," as we saw in our federal parliament when MPs Ken Wyatt and Linda Burney both gave maiden speeches wearing possum-skin coats. It is no different to Dutch people wearing clogs or the Irish diaspora dressing in green each St Patrick's Day. As Kipling said, "every nation, like every individual, walks in a vain show."

The economist and philosopher Amartya Sen has warned of the dangers of what he calls a "solitarist identity," which encourages difference that at best breeds misunderstanding and at worst violence, as our "shared humanity gets savagely challenged when the manifold divisions of the world are unified into one allegedly dominant system of classification." As a reporter I have seen the human debris from this clash of cultures, religions, civilisations and identities: think Hutu and Tutsi in Rwanda; Sunni and Shi'a throughout the Middle East; Hindu and Muslim in India and Pakistan; and Israeli versus Palestinian. Fundamentalists everywhere feed on the politics of identity: from right-wing political extremists (according to the 2015 Global Terrorism Index, the perpetrators of most terrorism in the West) to radical Islam associated with groups like al-Qaeda, the Islamic State or Boko Haram.

Sen says singular, overarching classifications can make the world "inflammable." Put simply: division breeds hate. Identity can be a source of warmth and richness, and it can add to a tapestry of difference that we can all share, or it can incite hatred, violence and terror. It was the belief in the superiority of a dominant European culture that wrought so much damage to the first peoples of this continent. I am attracted to Sen's idea of "layered identities"; in this way my Indigenous heritage forms a core part of my being, but I am also a man who speaks some Chinese, enjoys Italian food, is fascinated by international affairs and politics, and is at home living in the world's great cities.

In truth I was born a "young fogey," with an inbuilt natural reserve and conservatism. I don't like ostentatious displays; I prefer the quietness of my room, with my books and music, to the noise of the crowd. I admire stoicism more than flash. As a boy my ideal was the actor Sebastian Cabot in the television series *Family Affair*, with his courtly manner, three-piece suits and bowler hat, taking his daily constitutionals in the park; it is still how I imagine myself in old age. I love all things British: soft English rain, the green meadows, the barren moors: London with its lingering ghosts. English music has been the soundtrack of my life, from the bands I first fell in love with – the Beatles, the Stones, the Who and the Kinks – to my teenage obsession with the Jam and the Clash, and later the quintessentially fey Smiths. Can an Aborigine be a Smiths fan? I can be whatever I damn like.

I am a product as much, if not more, of the European Enlightenment (which belongs to all of us, not just to the West) as I am of the Dreaming. I value reason; the triumph of science over superstition; the universality of humanity. That I don't accept as fact the myth of the Rainbow Serpent doesn't make me less Aboriginal. I don't believe in a literal interpretation of Genesis either, but I can see the power of metaphor. I can see the beauty and power of the Dreaming stories – and of the Bible, the Koran, the Mahayana sutras, the Upanishads, and the *Iliad* and the *Odyssey*. I don't seek or need any endorsement from a community to tell me who I am; I don't try to profit from being Aboriginal – I take my skills and expertise to the marketplace, not my identity. I don't want to be put into any box; but rather, as Immanuel Kant said, to live free from "the ball and chain of an everlasting permanent minority."

As a journalist and writer, my freedom is precious – as Keats said, "the poetical character has no self ... the poet has no identity." I look to other writers who have bristled against dogma and rigid identity, such as the novelist Toni Morrison, whose work, she said, requires her to "think about how free I can be as an African-American woman writer in my genderized, sexualized and highly racialized world." The writer who, for me, most profoundly grapples with the puzzle of identity is the Polish Nobel laureate Czesław Miłosz. In his Nobel Prize acceptance speech he spoke of his "strange occupation" writing poems "in Polish while living in France and America." He described himself as a "child of Europe" but said there were two Europes and he was born into the one destined to descend into the "heart of the darkness of the twentieth century."

Miłosz conceded that he struggled to "distinguish reality from illusion." He was born in Lithuania, a country dominated and fought over by others. He described it as "a country of myths and poetry." He was a child of its land but not of its language; as such, he would always be regarded as a Polish, not Lithuanian, poet. "My family already in the sixteenth century spoke Polish, just as many families in Finland spoke Swedish, and in Ireland – English."

Miłosz contemplated his continent's history of violence and genocide and the legacy of silence. "Crimes against human rights never publicly denounced," he said, "are a poison which destroys the possibility of friendship between nations." He sought to give voice to that silence, to lay bare "memory like a wound," to write in a "dark age" but "longing for the Kingdom of Peace and Justice."

Miłosz tells me I am not alone. Like him, I was born into a country where my ancestral language was silenced; but just as he expressed himself in Polish, I have a love of English. The memories of wounds he spoke of are the memories Indigenous people share; our history is the history of others; those tyrants who reduced talk of genocide to a whisper in Europe find their equivalent in those who deny atrocity here. Each land has its own story, each people is unique, but the sweep of history gathers us all. Miłosz engaged in the world with all its beauty and horror in the same way as I seek to live in my world.

Why would Indigenous people today look to perpetuate potentially harmful divisions? Especially when those same divisions hurt us. Why would a young girl with a life of limitless possibilities hitch herself to separatism and victimhood? Why would she not look to find joy in a shared humanity? I see it as a terrible loss. My life has been enriched by friendships that span the globe. These are critical times; we need to ask fundamental questions: are we ready, capable and prepared to take up a place at the centre of Australian social, political and economic life? Is Australia ready to embrace the idea of a bigger country whose constitution reflects a deeper history than just the story of British settlement? In a world where the bonds of democracy are fraying, can our democracy encompass an acknowledgment of the sovereignty of first peoples? Must we lag as the only Commonwealth nation not to have a treaty with Indigenous people? A fuller discussion of this is beyond the scope of this essay, except to say that this isn't about separatism or assimilation, but rather about engagement from a position of strength and choice; as Amartya Sen says, with "the freedom ... in determining our priorities."

If ever I realise the gulf between me and other Indigenous people, it is today. I am sitting in a coffee shop in Broome. Elsewhere it is winter, but here the warm afternoon sun lingers into the evening. I am a face in the crowd, just another part of this great Australian mosaic. Around me there are tourists, a babel of languages, visitors drawn from around the world. They are having a remote Australian experience. They take chopper rides in the Kimberley; they camp out and eat under the stars; they giggle as their puffed cheeks threaten to explode trying to play the didjeridu; they take photos with black women in floral cotton dresses with big white-toothed grins; they will take home a rustic dot painting with a single-page note attached vouching for its authenticity and explaining its meaning. This is their Dreamtime wonderland, a picture postcard of "exotic" Aboriginal life.

The waitress brings my café latte and carrot cake. I am lost in thought, wondering about the future of the people I call my own. I am in town for a meeting of the Referendum Council, a body designed to consult with Aboriginals and Torres Strait Islanders on the best form of constitutional recognition. As laudable as the endeavour is, I admit that sometimes the whole exercise feels incongruous: asking Australians to recognise what is obvious. It is an issue heavy with symbolism, yet light on substance. Australians are notionally supportive. Yet Indigenous backing is not a given: some are vehemently opposed, preferring a treaty; others remain indifferent. On days like this the whole exercise can feel ludicrous.

Across the street in a park is a group of Aboriginal men. They are wiry and deeply black, with shocks of matted curly hair. They wear jeans stained with red dirt and checked polyester shirts; some have cowboy hats turned at the brim. There are a couple of women among them. Some are sprawled on the ground, others propped against trees. They are drinking, passing a bottle around. Two of the men stand and shape up. They swing wildly at each other. A few of the others stand between them, but they are drunk too, and can do little to stop the flailing fists. One of the men connects with the other's jaw; he stumbles backwards and there is a brief lull before the fighting begins again.

This is lunchtime entertainment. The tourists crane their necks to get a look. Shopkeepers step outside, shake their heads and wander back in. No one intervenes; it is all so familiar. Eventually a police van arrives; there is no urgency. The officers are young but not intimidated. This is entirely routine. They grab hold of the men, who drop their hands and passively stagger towards the van. They also know the drill. Each is bundled into the back and the young cops talk briefly to the others, who barely seem to register what is happening. The men will likely be taken to the local lock-up and put in a cell until they sober up.

This numbing scene is played out every day across the country. The Aboriginal writer Kevin Gilbert saw this a generation ago. In his 1973 book *Because A White Man'll Never Do It*, he describes his tour of outback New South Wales, painting a portrait of an urban Aboriginal society in decay, its people dislocated and estranged from their own traditions and the white towns they now lived in: "Underneath it all there is frustration, obsequious resentment, divided loyalties, uncertain values. There is no real belonging, no real identification except to misery. It is true that the modern Aborigine is sick, very sick."

Sitting in the Broome café, I had a flashback to an all too similar scene in a small NSW town twenty years earlier. I had been sent there as a reporter for the ABC program *Lateline*. My trip had been prompted by an Aboriginal Legal Service lawyer who warned that drinking and violence were so out of control there that within a generation an entire population could be wiped out. I had family there; my grandmother's family had been rounded up at the turn of the nineteenth century and deposited at small settlements throughout the state. Like all Aboriginal families, they had been forced to eke out an existence on repressive reserves or fringe camps. In my book *The Tears of Strangers*, I recalled an encounter in the local pub.

The two young girls propped up at the bar laughed easily and without inhibition. They threw their heads back and opened their mouths so wide you could see their tonsils vibrate. The more they drank, the happier they became. They had a cheekiness, a schoolgirl innocence about them. To me, and no doubt to themselves, they were indestructible. From the front bar of the main pub in town they could take on the world. They told me they were going to move away, go to the city, get married, have children and make a lot of money. The modest aspirations of city girls were the stuff of dreams to these two. Outside the pub was the grim reality they were chained to – a life of teenage pregnancy, boozing and brawling.

In the 1970s the Fraser government had invested in a new housing project. Malcolm Fraser himself had come to town to open it. I remember pulling the footage out of the ABC film library. As the prime minister toured the community, there were men drinking heavily, laughing and playing guitar. As part of my reporting I went back to that housing project:

> Now, I was standing in the wreckage of hope. The once pristine houses were gone, turned to firewood mostly. Black families lived five or six to a room, the old and young huddled together in makeshift tin shacks that bowed to the elements. I stepped over bodies as men slept off last night's hangovers, oblivious to me or my cameraman.

That generation did survive, in spite of the lawyer's dire warnings, but only barely. Today that same town has the lowest life expectancy in the country: less than forty years of age.

The opening scene of Warwick Thornton's 2009 film *Samson and Delilah* captures the quiet desperation and grinding monotony of remote community life. The male lead character, Samson, wakes to a soundtrack of country music; wordlessly he runs his fingers through his hair and pulls on the same dirty, wrinkled shirt he has no doubt worn the day before and the day before that. As the background song speaks of every day being a "sunshiny day," Samson reaches for a can of petrol, holds it to his face and inhales. Stumbling out to the morning, he finds his brother's band is rehearsing the one song it knows. In a moment of possibility and joy, Samson seizes the guitar, making a loud discordant sound, and a huge smile breaks across his face. His brother yanks the guitar from Samson's grasp and falls back in with the band's loping reggae one-song repertoire. The whole scene plays out in a matter of minutes, but it portrays an endless cycle of boredom, poverty and hopelessness. Thornton repeats the scene throughout the film, a reminder of Samson's alienation.

If only this were fiction – as bleak as it is, it merely hints at the reality for so many Indigenous kids locked out of the possibilities of life in one of the world's richest countries. In the film, after much pain, Samson finds peace and acceptance with the love of his girlfriend, Delilah. But life trumps art, and life is not given to such happy endings.

I am still haunted by the death of someone I never met but feel I know anyway. About to board an early morning flight from Melbourne to Sydney, I was listening to the radio news, which reported the suicide of a ten-year-old girl in the far-flung northern corner of Western Australia. I took my seat feeling numb. I took this tragedy personally; this was our failure, all of ours: a national shame. I wrote an article for the *Guardian* – it was the only thing I could do:

> Ten years old. Think about that. Someone's daughter. A child who came into the world with the joy of all newborns. A child who first smiled, who spoke her first words, who said "mum" and "dad." A child who laughed her first laugh, who took her first step, who held the hands of her parents as babies do: tiny hands gripping a finger ... think about that. Then ask: how can we possibly look away?

The girl was one of more than a dozen Indigenous people who took their lives in that same part of the country in less than three months. Her death is a reminder of a brutal statistic: Indigenous kids under the age of fourteen are ten times more likely to commit suicide than their non-Indigenous fellow Australians. I learnt later that she came from a family marked by tragedy, suicide, violence and alcohol abuse. As I wrote that day, "How many needless deaths does it take to tell us that Indigenous Australia is in deep, deep crisis?"

Just a few months later I sat with my son as he saw boys who look like him tear-gassed, beaten and bound to a chair in a hood. These were the boys of Don Dale, now known to all of us, but revealed that night on ABC TV's *Four Corners*. The prime minister responded in a matter of hours, calling a royal commission into the juvenile justice system in the Northern Territory, where more than 90 per cent of those in detention are black. As my son watched the television, I saw him lose his place in the world. His simple, uncomplicated belief in freedom and equality was shaken. Was this his country?

He has been raised in privilege, spending most of his childhood overseas. He has been to the best schools, is now studying at university and is a promising sportsman. His has been a life of possibilities – of opportunities far greater than those enjoyed by most Australian kids, let alone by Indigenous children. My son has been raised with a strong sense of his heritage and has deep and intricate kinship ties: he is an Indigenous boy – free to define that however he may wish. His life is so different from that of the boys he saw on the TV screen, and yet on a very personal level they are part of him. It could not but leave him puzzled and saddened. Here is the contradiction of the lives of people who identify as Indigenous; we are so few, we share a past, but our fates are so very different.

We have found a place in the Australian Dream. We are products of the same dispossession; my son's ancestors endured a similar history of injustice, exclusion and suffering to that endured by the forebears of the boys of Don Dale. We are products of Australia: its misery and its glory. Colonisation shattered the world of my ancestors. Dispossession and its impact – the legitimacy of settlement – remains at the core of our nation's unfinished business. Yet in 2016, on a personal level for me and my family, can I say the events of two centuries ago alone determine my fate?

The people of my grandfathers' generation – resourceful, courageous, hardworking – have inarguably set my life's course. The success of so many Indigenous people, overcoming discrimination, restrictive laws and segregation to synthesise the best of two traditions – black and white – should be seen as one of the pillars of Australian exceptionalism. The historian Geoffrey Blainey has made the case for the genius of Indigenous antiquity. He marvels at a people who navigated massive change: rising seas that shaped the continent and isolated the inhabitants for tens of thousands of years. For Blainey, this exceptional survival over tens of millennia grounds the Australian story that in time winds its way through the coming of the British and the economic boom of much of the nineteenth century to the creation of a democracy that stands as one of the world's oldest and most durable. The Australian experiment encompasses waves of immigration and the end of the White Australia policy, and the social, cultural and economic pendulum swinging from Europe to Asia. Writing in *Only in Australia: The History, Politics, and Economics of Australian Exceptionalism*, Blainey concludes of the nation: "What is the balance sheet? All in all, it is one of the most experimental, and one of the most exceptionalist, countries in the history of the modern world."

Blainey says the clash of British and Aboriginal cultures marked one of the sharpest contrasts in history. A people entering the Industrial Revolution confronted what he calls a collection of hundreds of "mini-republics," whose citizens did not read or write, who were not large-scale shepherds or millers or builders or metal workers; who had remained apart from the sweeping changes of the world. Here were two peoples – black and white – whose economic, political and social structures were entirely alien to each other. Of course it was devastating for the first peoples.

Yet it is wrong to think the Aboriginal contribution to this nation is confined to the deep past. The Indigenous experience bends and shifts with the growth of the country. In the midst of catastrophe, Aboriginal people were adapting to this utterly foreign intrusion. The survival and resilience of the descendants of the people of the Australian frontier should be seen as part of the pioneer mythology of this country. At Federation the Indigenous people were assumed to be dying out and would not be counted among the numbers of the Commonwealth. Now Australian law acknowledges native title, Indigenous people sit in our parliaments, and Indigenous art, music and dance have a unique, treasured place in our national culture. We may have rubbed uncomfortably against each other, but together we have enlarged the idea of Australia.

It is too convenient to imagine our lives bound to the fact of dispossession. Just as it does not solely determine my fate, nor does it explain the plight of the Don Dale boys or the ten-year-old suicide victim – not entirely. The fight for land rights has been a struggle to reverse dispossession. Today nearly a quarter of the Australian landmass is held under some form of Indigenous title. Across the country, Aborigines and Torres Strait Islanders hold land greater than three times the size of New Zealand. In some places, this is delivering better outcomes: cultural connectedness, entrepreneurial spirit, profitable mining royalty agreements and healthy self-determination, with robust and inclusive representation and dispute resolution.

Torres Strait Islanders are marrying land rights with economic and political autonomy. The Torres Strait Regional Authority administers its chain of islands through a twenty-member elected body that aims to strengthen the culture, society and economy of the people. Most of its funds go to developing jobs to break welfare cycles. On early morning walks around Thursday Island this year, I was struck by what a model Australian town it is: two cars in the driveway, boats, beautifully maintained lawns and gardens, two-storey houses, kids laughing and joking on their way to school. The Authority is the hopeful first step towards full Australian territory status.

In parts of the north, outstation movements offer a respite from an often-brutal life in town camps. Back on traditional country, communities are able to reassert models of authority and revive positive aspects of culture. But are they viable? The economist Jon Altman, in his 2010 paper "What future for remote Indigenous Australia?", says these places have developed a "hybrid economy": a synthesis of customary activity, market exchange and state support. He cites the Indigenous visual arts industry as one example of this. Altman rails against what he sees as a neoliberal project to close the gap by forcing Indigenous people into the mainstream economy. His hybrid model, he believes, offers a more culturally and socially secure future than the alternative of a precarious position on the economic ladder. Altman is suspicious of state attempts to transform people into "subjects of the global project of modernity, to become responsible citizens of a multicultural late liberal state, to be hard-working labourers or profit-driven entrepreneurs in a free market, to be capitalist consumers of mass culture."

Altman idealises Aboriginal people in remote communities living outside mainstream Australian life. He disavows the value of standard education for Indigenous children because they "live fundamentally non-standard lives." I find that baffling. Altman is an economist and anthropologist who has held a professorial post at the Australian National University: can he seriously be suggesting that an Aboriginal child would not benefit from, nor has the right to, the educational opportunities he has enjoyed? That they should not aspire to emulate his career? Would he rather they remain in "non-standard" but supposedly culturally "pure" circumstances? A fulfilled life, surely, is about enlarging the world of possibilities, and enriching social and cultural experiences. Why should Aboriginal children be denied the life-expanding potential of education: the wonders of Mozart, Einstein, Shakespeare, or, should they choose, Kanye and Kim, *Game of Thrones* and *The X Factor*, as well as an ongoing connection to a rich Indigenous cultural tradition?

My misgivings aside, Altman does correctly identify the complexity of remote communities. The trajectory of their engagement with a wider world is different to that of the more heavily and longer settled areas of the south. Elements of customary culture, economy and ways of life remain.

Never again miss an issue. Subscribe and save.

☐ **1 year auto-renewing print and digital subscription** (4 issues) $69.95 incl. GST (save 23%). Subscriptions outside Australia $109.95.

☐ **1 year print and digital subscription** (4 issues) $79.95 incl. GST (save 13%). Subscriptions outside Australia $119.95.

☐ **2 year print and digital subscription** (8 issues) $149.95 incl. GST (save 18%).

☐ Tick here to commence subscription with the current issue.

All prices include postage and handling.

PAYMENT DETAILS I enclose a cheque/money order made out to Schwartz Publishing Pty Ltd. Or please debit my credit card (MasterCard, Visa or Amex accepted).

CARD NO. ☐☐☐☐☐☐☐☐☐☐☐☐☐☐☐☐

EXPIRY DATE   /   CCV   AMOUNT $

CARDHOLDER'S NAME

SIGNATURE

NAME

ADDRESS

EMAIL   PHONE

Freecall: 1800 077 514 **or** +61 3 9486 0288 **email:** subscribe@blackincbooks.com **quarterlyessay.com**
Digital-only subscriptions are available from our website: quarterlyessay.com.au/subscribe

An inspired gift. Subscribe a friend.

☐ **1 year print and digital subscription** (4 issues) $79.95 incl. GST (save 13%). Subscriptions outside Australia $119.95.

☐ **2 year print and digital subscription** (8 issues) $149.95 incl. GST (save 18%).

☐ Tick here to commence subscription with the current issue.

All prices include postage and handling.

PAYMENT DETAILS I enclose a cheque/money order made out to Schwartz Publishing Pty Ltd. Or please debit my credit card (MasterCard, Visa or Amex accepted).

CARD NO. ☐☐☐☐☐☐☐☐☐☐☐☐☐☐☐☐

EXPIRY DATE   /   CCV   AMOUNT $

CARDHOLDER'S NAME   SIGNATURE

NAME

ADDRESS

EMAIL   PHONE

RECIPIENT'S NAME

RECIPIENT'S ADDRESS

RECIPIENT'S EMAIL   PHONE

Freecall: 1800 077 514 **or** +61 3 9486 0288 **email:** subscribe@blackincbooks.com **quarterlyessay.com**
Digital-only subscriptions are available from our website: quarterlyessay.com.au/subscribe

Delivery Address:
LEVEL 1, 221 DRUMMOND ST
CARLTON VIC 3053

Quarterly Essay
REPLY PAID 90094
CARLTON VIC 3053

Delivery Address:
LEVEL 1, 221 DRUMMOND ST
CARLTON VIC 3053

Quarterly Essay
REPLY PAID 90094
CARLTON VIC 3053

Land rights legislation and native title have transferred ownership of vast swathes of the north to Aboriginal communities. There, Indigenous Australians are a greater percentage of the population. In short, Aboriginal people in northern Australia are more visible, politically organised and land-rich, and more socially and culturally distinct from mainstream Australia.

Maria Lane's migration patterns – mobile communities emerging from segregated settlements to find a place in a wider Australian economy – fit less persuasively in the north than in her native South Australia. The historical forces that shaped the southern Indigenous economic migration have not existed to the same degree in the north. Strong cultural and social attachment may mean many Aboriginal people will be reluctant to move from their home country. Still, Indigenous prosperity is tied to the overall economic development of the north. Compared to the Aboriginal populations of southern Australia, who bore the brunt of European settlement and forced removal from land in the nineteenth century, Indigenous people in the more remote north could be in a stronger position to shape the direction of their lives. That should not mean shrinking from the world in isolated enclaves, but, ideally, engaging from a position of economic and cultural strength. Rather than being locked out of "standard education," an Aboriginal boy or girl should be able to look up at a passing passenger jet and dream of worlds beyond their own.

The anthropologist Nicolas Peterson has also looked at the challenges of remote Indigenous Australia. The outstation movement is an example of what he calls "Indigenous life projects," which seek autonomy beyond the market and the state. As he points out, though, this means acceptance of a lower standard of living. Peterson says that to achieve some measure of equality, to break cycles of dependency – to *close the gap* – "work – mainly in the form of selling labour – is going to be the lot of Aboriginal people as it is for the population at large."

Poor, remote communities remain vulnerable. Their crippling rates of disadvantage and associated societal dysfunction are hyperpoliticised and they are targets for state intervention. This is the world of the boys of Don

Dale: located between their communities, culture and the market; trapped in a cycle of misery. We find them in the worst statistics; their suffering reinforces and symbolises the sense of dislocation and injustice felt by Aboriginal people across the country. Their plight forms a bedrock of contemporary notions of Indigenous identity. Australians, meanwhile, remain perplexed: why can't things change? Why do we spend so much money for so little result?

"Mapping the Indigenous Program and Funding Maze," a Centre for Independent Studies (CIS) report, takes us through a litany of failure. The 2016 study found that total state and Commonwealth funding of Indigenous programs touches A$6 billion dollars a year (add indirect funding and it is substantially higher). Of more than a thousand programs, only 10 per cent are properly evaluated. Programs are run by ill-equipped, unqualified or uncommitted people and organisations. That has created an industry marked by a lack of accountability and transparency, which places Aboriginal people at the very bottom.

Just 20 per cent of the Indigenous population live in remote areas, but their disadvantage is so acute that it obscures the successful lives of others. The CIS report argued that we need to stop seeing the Indigenous community as a socio-economically homogeneous group and target more effectively those in greatest need. Mark Moran has spent many years as an aid worker overseas and in Indigenous communities. He has witnessed up close what Noel Pearson has called "the buffeting winds of policy." He says blackfellas have coined a term for this: "Serious whitefella stuff." It is the title of his book, which explores the failures of funding and practice, where people must "'make hay while the sun shines', 'bunker down' for the storms, take spoils when you can, minimise your losses, and be ever alert for the next policy wind to blow." Moran says this is a world "closed to most Australians' eyes." They glimpse it through the media's often shocking reports of abuse and neglect. An outraged nation demands action and Indigenous people elsewhere take to the streets protesting "another dispossession"; the cycle has become depressingly familiar.

We saw this in 2014, when the Barnett government in Western Australia announced plans to shut down more than 100 remote communities. Prime Minister Tony Abbott weighed in with the sort of ham-fisted comment that plagued his brief term as the nation's leader, saying the government couldn't "endlessly subsidise lifestyle choices ... not conducive to ... full participation in Australian society." Abbott had anointed himself Prime Minister for Aboriginal Affairs; he promised to sweat blood. He may have professed good intentions, but his was the approach of a truant officer. Indeed, Abbott would visit Indigenous communities and wander the streets, asking children why they weren't in school.

Tony Abbott, like each of us, is a product of his time, history and culture. His fondness for the days of Empire was never far from the surface (Knights and Dames). He claimed that Australia was "unsettled – or scarcely settled" before the British and that the arrival of the First Fleet was the nation's defining moment. It was clumsy and insensitive. But, by questioning the future of remote communities, Abbott had blundered into a critical debate, even as his choice of language inflamed and distracted from it.

We live in a globalised world. We are more connected than ever before. For the first time in history, more people live in cities and towns than rural areas. What future is there in isolation? For a decade I saw up close the power of the movement of people. China's economic boom drove the biggest human migration the world has ever seen. Hundreds of millions of people made their long march from the fields and remote villages to glittering new cities. A country that a generation earlier could barely feed itself lifted half a billion people out of poverty. I recall meeting one man who came to Shanghai with a suitcase and his dreams, and found work on a construction site. He worked overtime in exchange for offcuts of timber and discarded tools. In his spare time he set up a roadside stall selling his goods. When I met him, he was a millionaire with a small chain of hardware stores. I saw the grandchildren of peasant farmers win entry to the great universities of the world: Harvard, Oxford, Cambridge and Princeton.

I followed my own journey, my own migration. I had gone to China the son of an itinerant Aboriginal sawmiller, the descendant of black migrant fruit pickers who was now working for one of the world's great news networks, CNN. I returned to an Australia in the midst of its own economic miracle. We are enjoying our third decade of uninterrupted growth, yet we are reminded every day of the tragedy of unfulfilled lives in remote and impoverished black communities. They hang heavy with hopelessness. I recall a visit to Mutitjulu – a community in the shadow of Uluru and ground zero for the Howard government intervention in 2007. Then it was seen as a place in crisis: mired in drug and alcohol abuse, rife with allegations of violence and sexual assault.

I stood in the streets years later and saw little sign that the intervention had achieved much. The people complained of a loss of liberty, of government making decisions with no consultation or understanding of community needs. I saw people sitting aimlessly outside dilapidated homes. Grog was supposedly banned, but the ground was littered with shattered glass from discarded bottles of beer and spirits. Empty cans filled the inside of upturned cars. Peering into one, I saw the snarling carcass of a dead dog.

There is a palpable sense of disempowerment in these remote communities. The dead hand of officialdom touches every aspect of life. Contemporary policy is often predicated on imposing restrictions and managing personal responsibility. Government intervention often involves banning grog, reforming welfare, and controlling spending through smart cards. Of course this can be a circuit-breaker and a cathartic response to crisis. Aboriginal communities sometimes demand it. But it poses the question: what comes next? Intervention risks setting Aboriginal people apart: institutionalising their exceptional status, reinforcing powerlessness. As Moran says, "It seems that the government is prepared to use the tragic circumstances of Indigenous disadvantage to politically legitimise reforms not otherwise palatable to the Australian people."

These remote communities appear like a shattered mirror. If I look for my own reflection, I see only fragments. Each splintered shard reveals parts of Australia, of Indigenous society, of possibilities but no coherence. It is simplistic to tell people to get up and move, to threaten to withdraw government funding for "lifestyle choices." Those affected could see this as a "second dispossession," disempowering the people the government seeks to help. Alternatively, eking out an existence in "hybrid econo-mies" – shielded from "modernity" and the lure of consumer society – may preserve aspects of tradition or "culture" but entrench the economic gap and leave open the potential for demoralising intervention.

There is a battle for the soul of these communities. There are those who see them as archaic and redundant, in need of rescuing by the market and shoehorning into mainstream Australia. There are others who see virtue in the customary culture but have no ambition to see it become part of a modern, globalised world. I don't come from these communities. I look upon them with a sense of brotherhood but observe from afar and cannot claim any expertise. The solutions and leadership rest with the many strong, forward-thinking Indigenous leaders of the north – people like Northern Land Council CEO Joe Morrison, trying to chart a course between economic engagement and maintaining distinct and different cultural and value systems: how to stay black and prosper. He wants to build stronger, more accountable and better-governed communities while seeking real market opportunities to build wealth.

For now, the boys of Don Dale and so many thousands like them live in a shadow world of the Australian Dream: a nightmare played out on our television screens. Sitting in that Broome café, I have to remind myself that this is another Australia. In these Australian towns, kids are born into misery and sadness; there is death in these Australian towns. Watching the drunken fight, I could walk over and try to help – but, like the foreign tourists, I do nothing. The men in the park would look at me as though I were a foreigner anyway: I am an Australian, and between the café and the park is where one Australia ends and another begins.

THE QUIET REVOLUTION

> "Name a revolution that was started without your middle class?"
>
> — Warren Mundine

These are the things we don't talk about in Indigenous communities. These are our inconvenient truths. There is no single Aboriginal community. We are lacerated by class and gender and colour and geography. My life could not be more removed from that of the people in the park in Broome. Just how fractured we are was made plain by then Northern Territory MP Bess Nungarrayi Price, writing in In Black and White:

> The great majority of Australians who currently identify as "Indigenous" speak English, live in suburbs, and produce children with Australians who do not identify as Indigenous ... Many of them do quite well in the mainstream economy and society, supplying Indigenous Australia with its middle class and the majority of its spokespeople.

Price could well have been describing me. And I am not alone. The report "Mapping the Indigenous Program and Funding Maze" reveals that 65 per cent of Indigenous people in Australia (360,000) are employed and living lives, materially and socio-economically, like those of other Australians. This is three times more than the number living in urban and regional areas who are largely welfare-dependent (22 per cent). Another 70,000 people (13 per cent) are languishing in remote areas, also locked in cycles of dependence and welfare far from regular education or employment opportunities.

There is a story here, a story largely untold. It is a story of success and how it is spurned like an unwanted child. Indigenous lives have been framed by suffering. This resonates because it is rooted in fact. Our land was seized, our rights were extinguished, we were shot down and stricken with disease, our liberty was curtailed and our children taken.

Even writing this feels empowering, I have to admit – a victimhood I can hold over Australia. It is a story of injustice that explains residual anger. This is the "unfinished business" Bronwyn Carlson identified at the heart of black identity. History explains much, but, as the French historiographer Michel de Certeau said, it is only a trace of a trace. The very act of writing our histories is in itself a practice of falsification. They are facts arranged as a treatment for absence – a salve for loss. It is our attempt to make the world intelligible.

> Like Robinson Crusoe on the shore of his island before "the vestige of a naked foot imprinted upon the sand," the historian travels along the shore of his present; he visits those beaches where the other appears only as a *trace* of what has *passed*. Here he sets up his industry. On the basis of his imprints which are now definitely mute (that which is past will return no more, and its voice is lost forever) a literature is fabricated.

Anzac Day, Invasion Day: are they not each, in their way, our attempt to make the world intelligible? We render these memorials as quasi-myths to make a devastating loss more bearable. History, myth, memory and forgetting: these are the things of identity. For now, as I trace the footprints on the shoreline of my past, the marks of those who have come and suffered before, it is clear that I and hundreds of thousands of Indigenous people – to take up Certeau's Crusoe analogy – have emerged from the storm, washed up on our own uncharted island of black success.

Between 1996 and 2006 the Indigenous community was transformed. Numbers of educated, well-paid professionals exploded. In just a decade, they increased by nearly 75 per cent. That was more than double the increase in the non-Indigenous community. By 2006 more than 14,000 Aboriginal and Torres Strait Islanders between twenty and sixty-four years of age were employed in professional occupations. The government defines these jobs as analytical, conceptual and creative work in fields that range from the arts and media to engineering, education, health and the law. Put simply, we were using our brains as teachers, doctors, nurses, lawyers and journalists. These people comprise 13 per cent of the total Indigenous workforce. This still lags behind the general population, where the number of professionals is nearly 22 per cent, but the gap is closing fast.

Dr Julie Lahn from the Australian National University looked at this change in her paper "Aboriginal Professionals: Work, Class and Culture". She said, "Aboriginal professionals in urban centres remain largely overlooked." Lahn thought this was a major shortcoming that impedes a fuller understanding of the "processes of transformation which are increasingly evident to Aboriginal people themselves."

Some Indigenous people have begun to explore the impact of this Aboriginal middle class. They recognise it is a phenomenon that is met with suspicion, even hostility, by some in the Indigenous community. Larissa Behrendt, in an article for the *Guardian*, "Who's afraid of the Indigenous middle class?", sees a fracture in Aboriginal communities and politics between an old guard forged in anger and loyal to the power of protest, and a new generation seeking to "work within the system – to join the professions and participate in party politics – to seek to make change."

> The fracture seems reflective of so many divisions in indigenous politics, from opinions about constitutional recognition, to disagreements about the nature of welfare reform. While almost everyone can agree on the problems, the solution causes deep ruptures.

The rise of the Aboriginal middle class forms part of this fault-line. Behrendt herself is a Harvard-educated professor at the University of Technology, Sydney. She is an accomplished writer, publishing both fiction and non-fiction, a film-maker and broadcaster. She has emerged from a family history of forced child removal (her father part of what is now broadly – if still in some circles sceptically – known as the Stolen Generations) to a life of remarkable achievement. Behrendt is emblematic of this changing face of Indigenous Australia. It goes without saying that she is confident, but it is a quiet self-assuredness born of study in the library, not shouting on the picket line. She embraces glamour, invariably perfectly turned out in designer labels and teetering on impossibly high heels.

Behrendt is among those redefining what it means to be Indigenous. It is as much a rejection of black labels as it is of white stereotypes. This is a face seeping into the Australian consciousness, its arrival barely announced; suddenly, it seemed, it was just there: Jessica Mauboy on high rotation on music video channels and topping the charts, Miranda Tapsell clutching two Logie awards. Remember her speech? It won a standing ovation: "Put more beautiful people of colour on TV and connect viewers in ways which transcend race and unite us all." Hers is a powerful message and one that is becoming more common. It isn't about what divides us, but about how this nation can find itself in each other.

What more potent symbol was there than the 2015 National Rugby League grand final, when, for the first time, both teams were captained by Indigenous players: Johnathan Thurston with the North Queensland Cowboys and Justin Hodges leading the Brisbane Broncos? Both are self-aware Indigenous men conscious of their role beyond football. Thurston made a special call-out to the kids of the troubled Aurukun community after a Queensland State of Origin win, but when we see him regularly handing his Aboriginal-patterned headgear to a young white face in the crowd, we know he is making a powerful statement about reconciliation too.

Sport has always been a pathway to success for Indigenous Australians and celebrated in black communities. Indigenous people are unlikely to look askance at an incredibly wealthy Aboriginal athlete in the way they might a BMW-driving black accountant. Players such as Buddy Franklin, Eddie Betts and Cyril Rioli in the AFL and Greg Inglis, Sam Thaiday and Ben Barba in the NRL are household names. Indigenous people are fewer than 3 per cent of the total Australian population, yet comprise 9 per cent of players in the AFL. In the NRL, they constitute around 12 per cent.

Sporting stars may grab the headlines, but Indigenous people are also making their mark in less media-celebrated professions. There are around 30,000 Indigenous university graduates in Australia; in 1991 there were fewer than 4000. Those students who are breaking through are crafting a new narrative of empowerment and individuality. Dr Sana Nakata is a second-generation Indigenous PhD. Her father, Martin, was the first Torres Strait Islander to complete a doctorate, and his daughter finished hers in 2013. She is now teaching political theory at the University of Melbourne. She is part of a wave of Aboriginal and Torres Strait Islander students earning doctoral degrees. The number has quadrupled in the past twenty years. Between 1990 and 2000 there were fifty-five Indigenous students awarded PhDs; between 2000 and 2011 there were 219.

Speaking to the *Guardian*, Nakata drew the comparison with Indigenous excellence in the sporting arena: "Indigenous people can make great contributions off the sporting field. I would like the intellectual potential and contributions of Aboriginal and Torres Strait Islander people recognised." And she doesn't want to be celebrated simply for being an Indigenous person. Just as Johnathan Thurston is unquestionably one of the greatest Rugby League players – perhaps *the* greatest – so Nakata wishes to be judged on her professional merits. Her ambitions are not limited to the strictly Aboriginal sphere. "[I aim] to establish myself as one of this country's first Indigenous political theorists – first as a political theorist and an Indigenous political theorist second."

We are of one mind, if a generation apart. When I entered journalism, I made a conscious effort to avoid being typecast. I started as a copyboy for the *Canberra Times* – cutting a desultory and uninterested figure, frankly – washing cars, fetching meals and running text from desk to desk. I soaked up the last of the old smoke-filled newsrooms and irreverent old men with ink-stained fingers. It still surprises me all these years later that I managed to parlay that unimpressive and modest beginning into a cadetship with the Macquarie Radio Network, writing copy, attending press conferences, covering everything from fires to strikes to court cases. I graduated to the ABC and a position as a political reporter in Canberra. Through it all I tried to avoid covering Indigenous stories. It's not that I wasn't interested – I often suggested stories and encouraged others to tell them – I just didn't want to be marginalised.

I made the right call. At the risk of sounding immodest, I have had a thirty-year career in which I have covered the biggest stories of our time – the fall of apartheid in South Africa, the handover of Hong Kong to China, the death of Princess Diana, peace in Northern Ireland, coups and wars from Papua New Guinea to Iraq and Afghanistan, the rise of China and the paranoid reclusive regime of North Korea. I have reported from more than seventy countries and lived half of my working life overseas: in London, Hong Kong, Beijing, Abu Dhabi and Dubai. I am proud to say I have a mantelpiece of the most prestigious awards in Australian and international journalism. I would not have achieved that had I been identified solely as the "Indigenous reporter." The ABC has been recruiting and training Indigenous people for as long as I have been in journalism. At the time of writing, it is still to produce a single Indigenous foreign correspondent, Four Corners reporter or host of a prime-time national program. I suspect, though, that is about to change.

Larissa Behrendt bells the cat when it comes to the hard questions posed by this new form of Indigenous success: "How does a community that has partly been defined by its exclusion, disadvantage and poverty redefine itself? How does it increase its participation in the mainstream and not be assimilated?" Behrendt ultimately argues that a person's cultural identity should not be tied to poverty: "You are not more Aboriginal if you grew up struggling."

Easy to say, but Larissa knows as well as I that in the eyes of some we are "coconuts." The lawyer and activist Noel Pearson isn't as crude as that, but he has written warily of this new black middle class. A decade ago, in "Through the class ceiling," published in the Australian, Pearson warned of "the gulf between indigenous middle class and the rest of the mob." Pearson counts himself among this new professional, educated, high-earning group.

But, he says, the incomes and lifestyles of this new cohort, with its focus on individual achievement, contrast with culturally dense communities, with their "intense kinship and demand sharing." This can create a crisis of identity: "there is something slightly unpalatable or embarrassing about the idea of blackfellas being openly thought of as bourgeois."

Marcia Langton is blunt, forceful and unflinching on this topic. She has been the target of derision and vitriol and has seen others targeted:

> Those of us who are successful run the risk of being subject to abuse, accused of being "traitors" to our people, "assimilationists," and a number of other crimes against the natural order of things, as perceived by those who fail to understand their inherited racist worldview. I find myself explaining to young Aboriginal people who find it difficult to understand these opinions that many non-indigenous people, whether or not they pretend sympathy for the "Aboriginal problem," in truth prefer their Aborigines to be poor, drunk, drug addicted or in jail. If you don't conform to this stereotype then they may accuse you of lying about being Aboriginal "to obtain benefits." "Don't be fooled. Hold your head up," I say to them, and just get on with it. These detractors will never help you and they can only resent your success. They will become increasingly irrelevant as you become more successful.

In her Boyer Lectures of 2012 Langton spoke of trying to change the narrative "from the tired old story of the black victim/protester to a more informed account of Aboriginal engagement with modernity." She tied the growth of an Indigenous middle class to the Australian mining boom of the early 2000s. She conceded she had to confront the old trope of "Aboriginal people as the hapless victims of a voracious and brutal mining industry." It is important to point out that this trope took hold because it was often true. Western Australian mining magnate Lang Hancock wanted to sterilise blacks so they would breed themselves out (what an irony that several Aboriginal people claim to be Hancock's secret children!). In the 1980s Western Mining Corporation's Hugh Morgan mocked Indigenous spirituality and led a campaign against Aboriginal land rights, which he claimed threatened the mining industry. Three decades later the industry has not just survived, but thrived off the back of a rising China. Morgan has moderated his views and Langton – herself once a street-protesting firebrand – says we are trapped in an old binary of miners versus Aborigines. In her lectures she conceded there was work to be done in raising standards of negotiation and engagement, but said that critics of the resources industry remained "oblivious to twenty years of operation of the Native Title Act and refinements of other legislation." "It is little known that thousands of jobs for Aboriginal people and hundreds of businesses set up by Aboriginal entrepreneurs are just the tip of the iceberg, and there have been many other benefits."

It is beyond trite to suggest that a university degree and a job means someone is no longer – or less – Indigenous. Identity should not be means-tested. We must demand the right to define ourselves and what being Indigenous means. The new black middle class is developing its own consciousness. Some reject the idea of class identity, preferring to cling to race and referring to themselves as "just blackfellas." Others are embracing a cosmopolitan identity beyond "the mob." The members of this black bourgeoisie are just as likely as their white neighbours to be attached to the baubles and trinkets of conspicuous consumption; to trawl through Domain.com for their next investment, making the rounds of the Saturday auctions; they are just as likely to shop around for private schools; just as likely to book their holiday escape: that Disneyland adventure for the kids or the lazy Mediterranean cruise or the hideaway in the French countryside. This Indigenous middle class is not new; Australia has just not noticed. We are now seeing the second generation of Indigenous people strongly identifying, successful and self-determining, and the profound implications are being felt. To quote Marcia Langton, this is indeed a "Quiet Revolution."

GOING HOME

"The very time I thought I was lost,
My dungeon shook and my chains fell off."

— James Baldwin, *The Fire Next Time*

From the Oval Office to the mission football oval: in just two days I have traced the arc of my life. While my months-old speech is now the stuff of newspaper headlines, I have boarded one plane from Washington to Sydney, then another to Griffith: my hometown. I am driving with television presenter Julia Zemiro to film an episode of her program *Home Delivery*, a conceit built around a walk down memory lane. We return to the old Three Way settlement of my childhood, down the old roads I once walked to school, past my old house, crossing the irrigation channel where I would swim. I am swamped by memories and fight back tears. There are boys just like me – boys I grew up with, was related to, who didn't make it out; many are dead now, buried in the town cemetery. Time seems to fold in on itself and I am the young boys on bikes in the mission streets. How would they see me now? Greek-Australian comedian and actor Nick Giannopolous has spoken about returning to Greece and his cousins calling him "Kangarootha." In my way, I am a migrant just like Nick.

This is where the great Aboriginal migration led us. This is where my father's family ended up after walking off the Condobolin mission 300 kilometres away and seventy years ago. How much I owe them. They bundled together what little they had, lived on the outskirts of town and took their chances. They were following their ancestors, too. We were always migrants, part of modern humanity's trek out of Africa 100,000 years earlier. The people who touched these shores at least 60,000 years ago had made the first open-sea crossing in the history of humankind. My Aboriginal forebears fanned out across the continent, trading and building their own economies. They met the British settlers in conflict and cooperation, and endured dispossession, forced removal and segregation.

The assimilation era can be seen as a defining moment in the post-settlement history of Aboriginal people. *Terra nullius* and dispossession had set an unalterable course for the many hundreds of distinct peoples here who had made a home on this continent for tens of thousands of years. That catastrophic event, bringing disease and the gun, wrought more destruction in just a few decades than the millennia that preceded it. But by the 1930s Australia was a fact, and most people counted among the categories of Aborigines drew their ancestry from white settlers too.

Assimilation was about how the government tried to control this "problem," but it was also about how we negotiated this new reality. Assimilation was devastating for many: children were removed, people shamed into abandoning Aboriginal communities or culture. It is a mark of the strength of Aboriginal people that they not only endured this, but responded with renewed demands for equality and rights. The Aboriginal political movement found its voice, campaigning for full citizenship and jobs. As enforced segregation receded, whole communities hitched their wagons and moved across the country, as with the great dustbowl migration of America, or the post-war drift out of Europe. This was a quest for something better: a new beginning, new identities.

My mother and father took to the roads. With four children, they moved from town to town, my father always looking for work and a better life. They kept us together and took in others, reinforcing in me an abiding sense of kinship and connecting me to my history. I have followed their example, leading a nomadic life that has taken me around the world and back again. I am not unusual: I have met Aboriginal people in Israel, London, Beijing and Washington. We are more than an exception; we are the products of sacrifice and the promise of possibilities.

Yet the picture of Indigenous Australia remains predominantly bleak. The challenges can appear insurmountable, the disadvantage intractable. There is a north–south divide and widening class differences. The remote and poor are largely locked out of the economy, and hybrid economies, while allowing people to live on traditional lands, are limited in their capacity to generate wealth. Remote communities are heavily politicised, highly controlled and prone to intervention and impositions on their liberty. Maria Lane's Embedded Society is not always out of sight; it lives in our cities and towns, those people for whom the migration from the margins to the mainstream was not so profitable.

There is no shortage of "solutions" and "answers"; from those who say leave the isolated communities and join the market, to those who stress the need for "culture" and identity first: amorphous concepts that are often framed around opposition to economic development. Advocates like Noel Pearson speak of empowered communities, with agile individuals "orbiting": leaving for school and work, then returning or remitting money to relatives. The Chinese call these people "astronauts." The economic potential of native title and land rights has yet to be fully tapped. Some see a treaty or constitutional recognition (or, indeed, both) as providing a framework for greater self-determination and political representation. Lawyer Michael Mansell is reviving William Cooper's call of the 1930s for a separate Indigenous state. Some Aboriginal and Torres Strait Islander people are politically ambivalent and want nothing more than to be left alone: Australians with Indigenous heritage, but Australians no more or less.

One thing is undeniable: tens of thousands of Indigenous people are transforming their lives through their own efforts: they are doctors, lawyers, teachers, plumbers and film stars. As Maria Lane saw, this Open Society wants as little government intervention as possible in their lives; they are risk- and reward-oriented; they have mortgages, invest in superannuation and send their children to private schools. If that makes them sound like classic Liberal Party voters, it is because some of them most likely are.

This emerging middle class is part of the Australian mosaic, with heritage rich and diverse. Today the Indigenous community counts among its number those who also have Chinese, Lebanese, Russian, German, Greek and Italian ancestry. There are Indigenous Jews, Buddhists, Christians and Muslims. They can admire Picasso and Namatjira. They can speak French and revive Indigenous languages. These people are forging new identities and at the same time they are often comfortably Australian. The Open Society has closed the gap, while governments still search for inspiration.

Bill Stanner, the great anthropologist, believed that Aboriginal people were caught between the Dreaming and the market, two incompatible forces. It was a view that didn't account for Indigenous potential and ingenuity. He conceived then, as many anthropologists do now, of Indigenous culture as frozen in time, fragile enough to shatter on contact with modernity. My great-great-grandfather Frank Foster – a man forced from his land, expelled to faraway missions – endured the brutality of nineteenth-century colonisation and aspired to be a teacher. My grandfather worked in shearing sheds and orchards, fought in a war and fought for the rights of his people, and kept by his bed the Bible and the complete works of William Shakespeare; he was a man making two worlds one. Aboriginal people have maintained and enriched the idea of the Dreaming, and found a place in the market.

In 2011 two Indigenous women were involved in a vigorous exchange about the future of Aboriginal policy. Larissa Behrendt and Bess Nungarrayi Price are strong-willed, articulate and extraordinarily successful. But in so many ways they could not be more different. As we have seen, Larissa is a city-born lawyer and university professor, an urban aesthete. Bess has lived close to the earth, at the coalface of communities devastated by poverty, grog and violence. She is a woman in her fifties who has lost almost her entire family: dead before their time. Bess Price has also been a Northern Territory MP and a minister in the former Giles government. Bess is a conservative and strongly supported John Howard's 2007 NT intervention – a response to reports of rampant violence, addiction and sexual assault – while Larissa is a political progressive and was just as strongly opposed to it, concerned about the heavy hand of the state and attacks on the liberty of Aboriginal people. Here are two women who between them embody the full range of diversity in Indigenous society: politically, physically, socially and geographically. Larissa is a friend, whom I admire deeply; Bess, I have met only briefly but respect equally.

At the height of their debate, Price said something so direct, so simple and – to me – so devastatingly inarguable: "I want what she has for my children."

Patrick Lawrence

Like most writers with too much to do and insufficient time, I set out to skim
Don Watson's essay on the American political scene, seeking its gist and leaving
it at that. I soon gave up: there is too much to be missed in Watson's piece. This
is always the mark of excellent eyes and ears – these being the sine qua non of
first-rate writing.

I wish more Americans might see Watson's elegantly wrought rumination. It
is nearly always arriving foreigners who get to the pith of a people. Tocqueville,
who filled two volumes on America with exceptional insight after nine months'
travel, is the best-known example. The only Americans able to see as Americans
and also as others see them are returning expatriates, and, as Joyce more than
once noted, the exile gone home is punished savagely for all he sees and says.

Watson went after something deep and difficult during his time among Americans last summer, it seems to me. We are in crisis, let there be no doubt, but this
is far more profound than mere politics. One cannot possibly grasp the American
condition as we have it in the reports carried in the *Sydney Morning Herald* or the
Australian – or, still less likely, any American newspaper. They are not the right
technology, for we – we Americans – are amid a crisis in consciousness, to bring
it to a single word. The questions we face are psychological, having to do with
identity and who we think we are, as against what we have actually made of
ourselves. One must learn from Tocqueville, as Watson plainly has, and then set
out for that high, thinly populated ground where journalism and literature meet.
People such as Ryszard Kapuściński dwell there. It is where work that matters
gets done when the project is to capture a people and their society as in an
immense, panoramic Polaroid.

One way to get to the bottom of a place, paradoxically, is resolutely to explore
its surfaces and signifiers, and Watson has this, the semiologist's method, down
to an art. The mall-ified landscapes, the clapboard-and-green-shutters houses

that seem lost to the lives lived amid them, the downtowns that are "not entirely deserted but it feels that way," the beer-and-burger bars that seem like re-enactments, for Americans do not authentically gather anymore: perfect. In such evocations one grasps the vacancy of our public space and the emptied-out lives we live in consequence – we who bay incessantly about "community." Watson quotes Richard Ford to good effect: "It's really we who're threatened with not quite fully existing. It's we who're guilty of not having something better on our minds. It's our national malaise."

"We" is a fraught word among Americans. Nobody wants to own up to the mess we have made of ourselves and our country. It is always their fault – somebody else's, that "enemy within" in Watson's title. What passes for political process has been reduced to sheer spectacle in the way Guy Debord used this term. "We don't have politics in America," Gore Vidal once wrote. "We have elections." It is essential not to miss this: were Tocqueville writing today, he would have to choose another title: there is no democracy in America, and we, all of us, are responsible for this tragedy. This, it seems to me, is Watson's quarry.

Consider the evolution of mainstream reactions to Donald Trump's rise. When he first announced his candidacy, in mid-2015, he was dismissed as an entertainer. Then he was marked down as a passing political oddity, and then a kind of suicide bomber who would destroy the Republican Party from within but was of no interest to anyone else.

Things changed as the opinion polls began to indicate a very close contest between Trump and Hillary Clinton. Suddenly Trump is a threat to our national security and our very existence. Every derogatory descriptive in Webster's Third is hauled out and hurled Trump's way, usually more than once. It is all Trump, all horror, all the time. It grows tedious, to be honest.

There is something obsessive-compulsive in this. At writing (early October) it has come to resemble a Salem witch-hunt conducted – supreme irony – in the name of our liberal values. Supposedly liberal, I should say. I see two explanations, as follows.

One, few Americans – drifting as they do in the mainstream of opinion – want to see the "we" in the Trump phenomenon. Most of us are desperate to avoid admitting that the political culture that pushed Trump to the fore belongs to all of us and that many of us benefit from it just as it is. No, the Donald must be cast as some kind of "other" – along with his followers, of course.

The second point has to do with the matter of despotism. Watson dwells eruditely on fascism and those of its characteristics one may find in the Trump phenom. He is correct to do so – and correct again to dismiss the thought of a fascist order arising were Trump to be elected president. But he barely flicks at a political current that is just as pronounced, harder to see because it is everywhere, and arguably more pernicious. Tocqueville, in the second of his America books, calls it soft despotism. So can we.

American conservatives sometimes deploy Tocqueville's views on the "species of oppression" he so defined, so as to rip into the welfare state, federal regulation and other such right-wing obsessions. This is not my meaning. (And I question whether Tocqueville would accept it as his, either.) I refer to the oppression of the neoliberal order as consolidated in the post–Cold War period, notably during the triumphalist 1990s.

No threat of cataclysm in this, no Trump-ite catastrophe. "It would have a different character," as Tocqueville wrote presciently of this democratic despotism. "It would be more extensive and gentler or softer, and it would degrade men without tormenting them." This is the project of the end-of-history crowd: we are correct about everything, no need to think about it, and if you do manage to think a thought for yourself, it had better match ours. This is what I mean by perniciously dangerous, or vice versa.

As just implied, one of the most powerful features of neoliberal ideology is its intolerance of all deviation and difference. Abroad, one finds this at the root of our reigning Russophobia. At home, I see intolerance, various forms of prejudice, demonisation and the exploitation of fear – the last like shooting at the side of a barn, in the American context – at work in our Trumpophobia. This is the soft despotism of the American neoliberal. Hillary Clinton, to state the obvious, is the faith's high priestess.

Some mainstream Americans – meaning all who accept neoliberal thinking as a given, in no need of inquiry – prefer to pretend that the people Trump claims to speak for do not exist. It is easy enough, since mainstream-dwelling Americans rarely see them. Most, safe to say, are probably aware of their presence but find the thought that they should have a voice in the national conversation wildly unacceptable. Those people are to be confined to their "basket of deplorables," as Clinton artlessly but very succinctly put it this autumn. Among the most interesting questions posed late-ish in the campaign season is whether Trumpism will go away if he is defeated in November. Translation: can we resume ignoring them?

It is hard, honestly, to know how to apportion one's contempt in late 2016 America.

Return to Watson's blighted landscapes, desiccated towns and communities of the stupefied. All this we must lay nowhere but at neoliberalism's door. I see no alternative explanation of our fate. It is what a nation gets when it elevates market value to the only value – so surrendering to the corporatisation, commodification and marketisation of more or less everything.

Watson writes extensively of "malaise" in this context but never mentions "decline." This is another charged term in the American vocabulary. To be a declinist is quite unpatriotic. It puts one outside the tent urinating in, as L.B.J. would have put it. While many of our torments are mere indulgences, Americans' fear of decline is perfectly legitimate. This fear is the source of our malaise. Depression, I have long thought, arises out of feelings of powerlessness, and many of us understand that our corrupted political process renders us so.

I am not a declinist if this means I view the prospect as inevitable. The decline of America is possible, which is a very different thing. And it is a choice, even though most of us do not recognise it as one. Americans face many choices, and one might logically expect their magnitude to prod us into action. Just the opposite is the case: we have drifted so far from anything like an authentic political life, let so much go slack for so long, and so left ourselves with so much to do that the choices before us leave us paralysed. Which is to say the sensation of powerlessness is prevalent. The grim reality around the next corner, or the next, is that flinching from our choices in this way will amount to our choice, and decline will then await us: we will have chosen it.

Watson quotes Camus as wondering, "Shall I kill myself, or have a cup of coffee?" The attribution is common but mistaken, but we can leave this aside: Watson is wise to pose the question in his essay's context. To my mind we Americans have but one way forward. Let us begin with a good strong cup – our first order of business being, as Watson suggests, to awaken from our long, troubled sleep.

Patrick Lawrence

Nicole Hemmer

Don Watson's Tocquevillian journey through the United States is well suited to an election in which America seems a strange and foreign country, even to Americans. His explanation, which winds through the particularities of the present as well as the precedents of history, helps us better understand how, exactly, the wheels came off in 2016, and why so many Americans put their faith in a man so patently unqualified to be president.

To sharpen that picture, it would be useful to change the focus just a touch: to look at the present moment as one of historical change, and to find the roots not just of populism but of authoritarianism in America's past.

The twin campaigns of Bernie Sanders and Donald Trump point to a tectonic shift in American politics. For much of the twentieth century, the dividing lines were conservative versus liberal, right versus left. And those divisions remain: Sanders' supporters did not flock to Trump, as some analysts predicted they might. Not all populisms are the same. The populism that knitted together a racially diverse coalition of millennial voters in the Democratic Party does not have a natural tie to the nativist, racist populism of Donald Trump.

But that left/right cleavage is being overrun by anxieties about globalisation, the economy, civil liberties and foreign policy. The Republican Party, in particular, has been splintered by these forces. In the aftermath of the 2012 election, party elites made immigration reform a central item; they were smacked down, brutally, by their base. Libertarianism blossomed briefly as a wave of non-interventionism rippled through the party; by the end of 2013, the rise of ISIS had shoved the pendulum back towards muscular militarism.

All the while an anti-establishment populism simmered. Opposition to the Obama presidency kept the anger directed at the Democrats, holding together a fracturing Republican Party. The Tea Party had plenty of anger at Wall Street, a traditional GOP stronghold, as well as at corporations and elites. Party leaders tried to corral that anger, but with no platform to bind the grassroots to the leadership, the party's politics devolved into reckless obstructionism, shutting down the government, playing brinksmanship with the economy, and hobbling the Supreme Court.

The 2016 Republican primaries showed what happened when that obstructionist bond was removed. Carefully groomed candidates fell, one after the other, to an angry populist whose policy preferences had little to do with the conservative coalition that once provided the foundation of the Republican Party. Trump rejected free markets, neoconservatism, right-wing social issues, small-government orthodoxy. On issues of racism, he put down the dog whistle and picked up the bullhorn. In less than a year, he laid waste to the party of Reagan.

Bernie Sanders represented some of those same forces shuddering through the Democratic Party, but the Democrats have long been more a coalition of interests than a party of ideas. Hillary Clinton could absorb Sanders' critiques, turning up the dial on regulation, backing off from the Trans-Pacific Partnership. The party is shifting, but is managing the pivot more smoothly than the GOP, where Trump has gone to war with the party establishment. For Republicans, the enemy truly is within.

The United States is in the midst of a massive political transformation, one that has given rise to an unprecedented candidacy. Unprecedented in the most troubling ways: a candidate who threatens to jail his opponent, who argues the coming election is rigged and invalid, who is seen by the vast majority of Americans as unqualified for the presidency.

Yet while Trump's breaks with precedent are vitally important, so too are the ways he echoes old tendencies. The history of populism that Watson sketches is critical to understanding the appeal of Trump's message. But let's add to that another history: a history of distrust in democracy, along with an American approval, from time to time, of authoritarianism.

The modern presidency, marked by candidate-driven campaigns, emerged at the start of the twentieth century with Teddy Roosevelt. Roosevelt wanted an expansive, muscular executive – he's the one who christened the presidency "the bully pulpit" – and he readily seized opportunities to expand the scope of his power. So impressed was he with his abilities as president, and so unimpressed with his successor, that in 1912 he broke with tradition and ran for an unprecedented third term. His decision hinted at the ways personality and power were coalescing to strengthen the office of the presidency.

When the nation careened into economic crisis in the early 1930s, the danger of that growing power became visible. The crisis revealed a longing for an authoritarian, a single person who could fix what seemed so stubbornly resistant to fixing. Taking office, Franklin Delano Roosevelt asked for "broad executive power" and Congress granted it. The word "dictator" was used, and used approvingly. Walter Lippmann told Roosevelt, "You may have no alternative but to assume dictatorial powers." The *New York Herald Tribune* met his inauguration with the amenable headline, "For Dictatorship If Necessary."

Roosevelt was no dictator, but he did believe he was specially suited to meet the crisis. And so he grabbed for unprecedented powers, including control of the economy and of the Supreme Court. He was granted the first and rebuffed on the second. And as the nation was drawn into war with Europe, he repeated his cousin's big power play: he ran for – and won – a third term, and then a fourth.

Roosevelt played by the rules. He asked Congress for power and retreated when refused it. He did not seize the presidency; he asked the American people for their votes, which they granted. But his long tenure in office revealed that Americans in times of crisis hungered for an authority figure to tell them what to do. They longed for it. Those that didn't favour Roosevelt turned to the anti-Semitic preacher Charles Coughlin or Louisiana's Huey Long. They sought a strongman.

This was before the anti-authority turn in American culture. In a way, though, the trends of the past forty years have helped set the stage for a figure like Trump. Americans have lost faith in the institutions of civil society: government, media, school, court. They greet with suspicion the sort of authority that comes with the imprimatur of organisation – a sign that for many Americans, there is an open breach with their communitarian side.

Which is what makes Trump's candidacy so interesting. He is an authoritarian figure whose power derives from a sort of radical individualism. Having lost trust in institutions, his supporters turn to a single man with no loyalty to any community or institution or party or nation.

There is an absence in American national culture that Trump fills like a malignant growth, a diminished civil society too stunted to counter the fear-based politics that Watson decries. The great task of the next generation is to rebuild a shared faith in – and commitment to – the institutions and ideas that are the special genius of the American system. In the course of that rebuilding process, the American people have a chance to recover not the country's greatness, but its goodness.

Nicole Hemmer

Bruce Wolpe

If you are reading this and Donald J. Trump is the president-elect of the United States, we will, thanks to Don Watson, know why.

Nearly two centuries after the appearance of *Democracy in America*, Watson is within the august penumbra of Alexis de Tocqueville and, for contemporary tragics of the American experience, on par with AdT's twentieth-century heir, BHL (Bernard-Henri Lévy), whose *American Vertigo* a decade ago similarly made sense of America and its place in our universe. For this, we are greatly indebted. Watson is the keenest observer, scholar and analyst.

Indeed, if Trump wins – an increasingly unlikely prospect in mid-October – it will be because of what Watson found in his journeys, such as to Janesville, Wisconsin, unknown, we dare say, to 99.999% of Americans, much less the world, until now, with the ascension of its Member of the US House of Representatives, Paul Ryan, to become Speaker, the third-highest constitutional office, and clearly an aspirant, in a post-Trump world, to the presidency itself.

Watson writes of Trump's appeal:

> Trump says, Hand your fear over to me. Hand your loathing over too. I will deal with your enemies as I have dealt with mine. I will give you back your freedom, and your country. Your old lives will be yours to live again. I will halt the terminal decline. American exceptionalism, in which you all hold shares, will be underwritten by an exceptional American.

If only the Donald could read that from a teleprompter and stop getting up at 3 a.m. to attack a former Miss Universe on Twitter. Or get into a fight with the Pope. Or impugn a Vietnam War hero and prisoner-of-war. Or stomp on the grief of an American Muslim family whose son sacrificed his life to save fellow American soldiers in Iraq. Or disparage the integrity of a judge because his parents were from Mexico. Or raise the implicit spectre of unleashed vigilante gun violence against his opponent.

As Watson shows us through his wonderful reporting, a good part of America is ripe for Trump's message. The anger and frustration of less-educated white men in particular, whose lives have been harmed by economic forces they do not understand and that are beyond their control, who see the country becoming strange to their eyes as its demographic face changes in their lifetimes, who rage against an Imperial City that is dysfunctional, obsessed with itself and its power, greedy and unresponsive to their needs – Watson brings this home to us.

Any Republican candidate can tap into this – and, indeed, the ticket the Democrats feared most was Senator Marco Rubio of Florida and Governor John Kasich of Ohio. They would have been on-message for the angry populist cause, and formed a potent generational, cultural and ideological force to go up against Hillary Clinton. But alas, a split field of fifteen could not stop a determined authoritarian narcissist from his hostile takeover of the Republican Party – his biggest business deal ever, and a massive expansion of the Trump brand. Could be worth billions.

For all of this that Watson chronicles so well, there remains a nagging question. It is not about Trump's pedigree. His political identity contains many slivers of American extremism and radicalism: Huey Long, Charles Lindbergh, Joe McCarthy, George Wallace, Barry Goldwater, Pat Buchanan, H. Ross Perot. In this mix lies the demagoguery, the racism, the isolationism, the protectionism, the pugilism, the crony capitalism that defines Trump.

The nagging question about Trump is not about his psychological infirmities, which David Brooks has explored in the *New York Times*, and which many learned medical practitioners will assess in books yet to be written.

The nagging question about this horrible and dangerous man is: how has he been able to persist in a parallel universe in which the normal laws of political gravity do not apply? Where he can say and do the most outrageous and unacceptable things and not be driven from the race? (As a contrast, can you imagine what would have happened if, in 2008, Senator Barack Obama had said at a political rally where some were demonstrating against him, "I want to punch that guy in the face"? He would have been called an uppity racial epithet and been driven from the race within a day.)

Trump commits these political atrocities all the time – and survives. To his tens of millions of supporters, these acts seem not to undercut his legitimacy as a presidential candidate. Why is that?

An explanation may well lie in our culture. In fact, as Trump seeks the West Wing, it may be said that the Trump problem we face began with *The West Wing*. Aaron Sorkin's magnificent and magisterial fictional creation of a modern American presidency brought home to tens of millions a demystified – but heroic – White House. It showed us inside the Oval and the Situation rooms, the Lincoln Bedroom and Air Force One, the limo and Camp David, and displayed all the high-intensity people and their purposes, and the toys that make the functioning of the modern presidency possible. It was wildly popular. Indeed, the series has a cult following, even in Australia, and has spawned other shows that have also brought to tens of millions more people, over two decades, the reality television view of Washington: *Scandal, State of Affairs, Commander in Chief, Madam Secretary, Veep, Homeland, 24 . . .* and *House of Cards*.

The theory posited here is that *Donald Trump the Presidency* is and reflects this declension – that the Trump candidacy is the bastard descendant of *The West Wing*: that if a real-life candidate appears, with cunning theatrical skills, who has all the presidential accoutrements – the airplane, the chopper, the entourage, the luxury playgrounds, the command over media and television networks, the omnipresence in commentary and analysis – that by having all these stylistic elements of presidential power, millions of people can indeed see, because they have seen it for years on television – and not just heroic versions of the presidency but revolting and perverted depictions of the presidency, such as in *House of Cards* – that yes, that man Trump could be President of the United States. Who today can know that Frank Underwood would never make it to the White House?

The primal intersection of the Trump parallel universe with the real-world presidential campaign was the "birther" moment in 2011, when the Trump helicopter landed in New Hampshire (gee, looks just like Marine One landing at Camp David! And with breathless wall-to-wall live cable TV coverage of the event!) and Trump took credit for the release of President Obama's birth certificate. From that moment in New Hampshire, he – and we – were truly off to the races.

And five years later, Trump shows no contrition, makes no apology, for a racist canard designed purely to undercut the legitimacy, for Trump's supporters, of the first African American president: was Obama really an American by birth and eligible to serve? And still today Trump lies about a tie between the "issue" and Hillary Clinton, a lie he uses to justify his original pursuit of the "issue."

In September, the *Washington Post* was told by Leonard Steinhorn, a professor at American University who is teaching a course on communications and the election:

> He [Trump] had a lifetime of experience with TV, and he understands the power of the medium in a way that many presidents have not. Donald Trump set out in this campaign to dominate the [TV] experience, to keep people glued in and to define the parameters of how we all experience this election.

The context, the echo chamber, for today's Trump reality show is a rich cinematic library. In addition to the TV series, we are seeing this man through the lens of a panoply of motion pictures whose actors exhibit presidential virtues, save the country, and sometimes the planet: *The American President*, *Air Force One*, *Independence Day*, *Deep Impact*, *Primary Colors*, *Dave*, *In the Line of Fire*, *White House Down*.

To be sure, we see the real-world White House for what it is. But as we are seeing it, we are seeing it through the lens of our entertainment culture. What does everyone say after they see a terrible, violent tragedy in real life, such as a terror attack, a building exploding, a bridge collapse, an airplane crash? "It was just like a movie." No, it was just like real life.

So the issue is not just that the Trump candidacy resembles a reality television show – something President Obama strenuously called to account in May:

> This is a serious job. This is not entertainment, this is not a reality show. This is a contest for the presidency of the United States. What that means is every candidate, every nominee needs to be subject to ... exacting standards of genuine scrutiny.

The answer to the nagging question of Trump and why he has got this far, and is only one vote away from becoming president, is that America's entertainment culture, in the way it portrays the presidency, legitimises even a Donald Trump as a serious contender for the highest office in the land.

As Obama's former speechwriter Jon Favreau told the *New York Times* in September:

> I worry that if those of us in politics and the media don't do a lot of soul-searching after this election, a slightly smarter Trump will succeed in the future. For some politicians and consultants, the takeaway from this election will be that they can get away with almost anything.

Trump's secret to success is not simply being identified with celebrity. Presidents have associated with Hollywood and entertainment since motion pictures were born. In modern times, to cite a handful of examples, Kennedy hung out with Marilyn Monroe, Peter Lawford, Dean Martin and Sammy Davis Jr. Ronald Reagan, an actor himself, was close with Sinatra, Elizabeth Taylor, Jimmy Stewart and dozens of Hollywood moguls and powerbrokers. Clinton with Streisand and Sheryl Crow. Obama with Beyoncé, Oprah, Stevie Wonder, Paul McCartney and so many more.

The issue is not presidential candidates and celebrity. The issue is not reality television. The issue is a culture that has corrupted our view of politics to such a point that perhaps 45 per cent of the country cannot distinguish the virtues of a Trump and a Clinton.

That is our problem.

So what's the answer? Aaron Sorkin's team knows what to do. In September, the cast of The West Wing campaigned for Hillary in Ohio. Thank you, President Bartlet! Surely you will prevail again, so that your successor in the Oval Office is worthy of the job and the trust of the American people. This is what it comes down to. A key swing state swayed by the cast of The West Wing. A cultural legacy redeemed.

As Don Watson sincerely hopes will be the case.

Me too.

Bruce Wolpe

Dennis Altman

I am writing this in the aftermath of the first presidential debate, which common sense suggests Hillary won convincingly. But as we know, rationality no longer plays much part in elections, and the incessant news cycle means my comments will inevitably be out of date when you read them. Anything I might say about *Enemy Within* will either seem naive or prescient, depending on the outcome of the election.

Like Hillary Clinton, Don Watson desperately wants to believe in America: it is, he tells us, "a miracle of an ever-evolving pluralist democracy and ... the last great hope of humankind. It is a wonderland of invention, a marvel of freedom and tolerance, and by most measures the greatest country on earth."

Like Bernie Sanders, he then itemises all the problems and defects that undermine these claims, especially massive inequality – four times the incarceration rate of China – and the overwhelming impact of money in politics. He doesn't discuss the recent "evolution" of the political system, which has led to systematic gerrymandering of elections to the House of Representatives and could ensure Republican control even in the face of a major Democratic vote this November.

The emphasis of the subtitle of this essay is revealing: "American politics in the time of Trump." Hillary Clinton remains the more likely future president, but she receives little attention in this essay, which is concerned with explaining the unlikely appeal of Trump, who both appals and fascinates us all. Like others caught up in a bromance with Bernie Sanders, Don's support for Clinton is at best grudging – her election is necessary to block Trump – and ignores that millions of Democrats backed her in the primary because they actually want her as president.

Don explains that he focused his essay on Wisconsin to avoid the clichéd bastions of either the liberal coastal cities or the redneck Deep South: "a normal sort of place." His description of Wisconsin rightly includes the poor and largely African American centre of Milwaukee, but he hardly lingers there, and the bulk of the essay reflects an America that is overwhelmingly white and torn between progressive and conservative traditions.

By largely ignoring non-white Americans, Don fails to convey the strong support for Hillary, and why Bill Clinton was regarded by many as "the first black president." There are good reasons for progressives to criticise Hillary: her closeness to major corporate interests and her record on foreign interventions among them. But there are also positives in her record, largely overlooked by those who look back longingly at the quixotic hopes of Bernie Sanders to capture a nomination he was never seriously likely to win.

Don ends his essay by describing Hillary as "a foreign policy hawk with no demonstrated ability to think beyond the doctrine of exceptionalism." It is true that as Secretary of State Clinton is known to have favoured a more interventionist position on several crucial issues than did President Obama. But two questions arise: was she always wrong? And has she learnt from those areas where intervention proved disastrous? Maybe Clinton was right to push for stronger US involvement in Syria, to have wanted the United States to impose a no-fly zone before Russian and Turkish involvement made this impractical?

Whether she realises that much American intervention in the Middle East has been, at best, counterproductive is hard to assess, as it is hardly the stuff of campaign oratory. Both Trump and Sanders played on the weariness that most Americans feel after almost two decades of military interventions – Afghanistan, Iraq, Libya – that have only fuelled instability and disaster. Let's hope that Clinton shares some of this scepticism and is willing to learn from past mistakes.

Dennis Altman

David Goodman

I have been travelling in the United States since mid-August and caught up in observing this can't-look-away-from-it, disturbing and fascinating election. Each day brings something new – most of it initiated somehow by Donald Trump. In some ways it is a miracle there is anything fresh to say about the election, but Watson's essay succeeds – it was a joy to read, both for its larger arguments and for its abundance of astute passing observations. This on the Tea Party, for example – "It's useless to tell them that people are free in many other countries as well, and free from worrying about freedom so much, many of them" – came back to me the other night, hearing CNN's London correspondent explaining how difficult the Trump fiasco has been for her to explain in Europe, where people, she said, look up to the US as the home of freedom.

The presidency arguably gets too much attention: both inside and outside the US, the media focuses on the presidency and the presidential race to the exclusion of most other forms of American politics and government. That is most true of the febrile US cable news channels, on which there has been almost no other story since the primaries began in February. This reflects the weakening of local news everywhere. In the political economy of contemporary media, stories about global celebrities have the highest value because they are saleable worldwide, while local coverage has become an expensive luxury; the *Washington Post* reported in 2014 that "the economics of the digital age work strongly against reporting about schools, cops and the folks down the street." That is only going to get worse. Stories about Donald and Hillary fill so much media space – MSNBC this morning, for example, reporting each tweet Trump sent off as it happened. This presidential race has been so absorbing, so impossible to turn off, such great theatre, that it will only increase attention on the presidency, which will in the end produce more frustration. The power of the United States derives from its size, but its size and diversity make the choice of a generally admired leader an almost impossible task. This time around, so many hours of attention and thought and analysis have produced, as so many comment, the most unpopular candidates ever. The increasingly overwhelming stress on the presidency makes for exasperation and disappointment all round – presidents who don't control Congress (and that is most of them) can only do so much.

Importantly, Watson sets this depressing, entrancing presidential race in the context of American government more broadly. His portrait of Hillary's Planned Parenthood speech evokes some of the best aspects of the US democratic culture: "Organising around an idea or a cause, networking, lobbying, educating, publicising, protesting and pushing into representative politics to change the world from within – these are American democratic traditions." He journeys to Wisconsin and appreciatively explicates the progressive "Wisconsin Idea" of education and government in service of the state and its industries. There is something almost Australian about Wisconsin progressivism – that optimistic and experimental sense of the state as a social laboratory. Remembering that tradition, talking as Watson does to successful mayors and state legislators, is one important antidote to the political ennui induced by too great a fixation on the presidency.

There have been few policies debated in this presidential election, particularly since the primaries, unless you count the wall. So much of the coverage (even, or perhaps especially, on the specialist political news channels) has been about personality and morality – are these good people? Sometimes, despite everything, that turns into a discussion of policy and principle. The pursuit of Trump's tax record, for example, began as a political tactic, but ended in something of a national debate about public and private wealth – an issue that has preoccupied Americans since the beginnings of the republic.

Of course, the presidency still matters a great deal. Watson's question is about what makes Trump possible. He gives an excellent account of the frustrations that have fuelled Trumpism: the increasing wealth divide, the sense of loss of status and entitlement. When Watson says of globalisation that "what enriches one tribe impoverishes and threatens another," he is perhaps conceding some truth at the heart of this political movement. It is the mere evocation of the problems that works politically – Trump's proposed solutions remain almost entirely vague. Still, the willingness to believe in him astonishes. An otherwise observant, well-informed taxi driver in Virginia cautiously edged around to telling me she was for Trump because of Hillary's active support for terrorism. A sixty-something waitress in North Carolina, the morning after the release of Trump's lewd 2005 bus discussions, glanced at the TV and sighed, "Poor Donald."

Watson carefully identifies Trump's following as in general white (his support among African Americans currently hovering between 0 and 1 per cent). But Sanders' ardent support was also identified by analysts as "too white to win." Another reason the most enthralling theatre of this campaign might not be a glimpse of the future is that the 2016 race has failed to throw up either compelling inheritors of the Obama coalition or skilled shapers of other multiracial alliances.

Maybe I would disagree that "Americans are divided on party lines as never before." Party conflict has often been fierce, most of all when the party alignments coincided with racial and other divides. Was there once a more civilised partisanship? On the one hand, some – maybe many – Americans believed the story that Franklin Roosevelt was not a real American, but rather a Jew called Rosenfeldt. Earlier in the Trump candidacy, commentators pointed to his probably unconscious evocations of 1930s/40s isolationism. But on the other hand, the key isolationist figures of that period look substantial, knowledgeable and principled compared to Trump. Charles Lindbergh said in 1941, "We believe in an independent destiny for America," but immediately added: "Such a destiny does not mean that we will build a wall around our country and isolate ourselves from contact with the rest of the world." Lindbergh made his racial views explicit, rather than relying on innuendo.

There is a body of explanation going back to the 1980s about working-class conservatism and there is perhaps a danger of subsuming Trumpism into these more familiar paradoxes. Trump is not Thatcher or Reagan; he is not a conservative in their mould at all. He has, to be sure, gone along with tax cuts for the wealthy, but that is not the most energising issue for him or his supporters. He seems, in fact, to be a big-government man, judging by the number of "magic wand" promises he makes. All the problems that will vanish when he is elected (urban crime, unemployment, economic competition with other nations) will do so because he will use the powers of government to fix them. He does not like free-trade agreements, threatening Ford with punitive tariffs if it moves more manufacturing to Mexico: "We're gonna charge them a 35 per cent tax. And you know what's gonna happen, they're never going to leave." No wonder Rush Limbaugh lamented in September, "I wish conservatism was on the ballot."

David Goodman

Patrick McCaughey

Don Watson is good at skewering American embarrassments, most notably "American exceptionalism" and the "American Dream." For the past three decades I have lived in the US and still cringe when I hear the political classes call America "the greatest nation on earth." This is even more awful when one is confronted with the spectacle of American inequality, persistent discrimination against minorities and women, and endemic gun violence. The American Dream seems an unbreakable bubble. The belief that everybody can rise and become rich if they simply "play by the rules, work hard and pay their taxes" is like a divine mantra. How can any politician say such things when the administration struggles to establish a minimum wage of $15 per hour? If you do the math, that would barely bring you over the poverty line if you worked a forty-hour week.

Cognate to these embarrassments is the persistent belief that a failure in "leadership" has robbed America of its greatness, its exceptionalism, and denied its struggling citizenry the fulfilment of the Dream. The weakness of Barack Obama and the need for a strong leader became the rallying cry of the Republicans in 2016. To their horror, Donald Trump emerged in that role. Hillary Clinton was denied it because she is a woman and a self-serving career politician.

The left like to throw the word "fascist" around on such occasions. Mitt Romney or Newt Gingrich, fascists? Hardly. Trump comes closer to wearing that Halloween costume. Watson is rightly measured on the topic, but the following words and actions would make the most moderate pause:

- **Discredit the judiciary:** Trump has claimed and never revoked the statement that the Mexican parentage of the federal judge hearing the case against Trump University should disqualify him.

- **Muzzle the press:** Watson's vignette of the Republican campaign corralling the press at Trump's rallies at the back of the room to make them a clear object of mockery to the crowd smacks of more than intimidation. Trump banned journalists from the *Washington Post* from travelling in his official press entourage.

- **Deploy the state against the individual:** Trump has threatened to use the engines of the state to intimidate and harm individuals who oppose him. The most obvious case is that of Jeff Bezos, founder of Amazon and proprietor of the *Washington Post*. Life would not be so easy for Amazon if I became president, so Trump mused to the press.

- **Persecute a minority:** Trump has overtly threatened a minority by claiming he'll deport undocumented Latinos and their children, and also threatened to isolate Muslims in American society, who are portrayed as a perpetual threat from within.

- **Demonise foreign powers:** The threat from without is a common thread in totalitarian ideology and behaviour. Trump has demonised "Jina", as he calls the People's Republic. Once again, only the Strong Leader can prevail against such powers.

- **Prey on women:** The revelations following the release of the *Access Hollywood* tape about Trump's sexual mores and behaviour strongly support the claim of his belief in the superiority of man, the Übermensch, now as reality TV star, who must have his way with women.

The drive and effect of these elements in Trump's campaign have created the fearful electorate. Watson is very good on this: "Americans, who once admired courage above all human qualities, now seem to get high on fear. Not that we see them trembling; but we see and hear fear's most common disguise, belligerence."

Fear is contagious. African American communities are more deeply fearful of the police – of the forces of law and order in general – than ever in the post–Martin Luther King world, even when there are many African American cops on duty in the inner precincts of America's troubled cities. Every month, unarmed black men are shot and killed by police. It's as though the police can't help themselves, knowing full well the dire consequences of such shootings – from triggering major communal riots to instigating federal investigations by the Department of Justice, to say nothing of individual prosecutions for manslaughter, and even murder. Trump promises to encourage "stop and frisk" policies, even though they have been ruled unconstitutional. Such a policy is rightly seen as the perfect way of intimidating African Americans. Any black man in a car driving through a white suburb or area is liable to be stopped, told to get out of the car, and shaken down by a police officer ostensibly looking for drugs or illegal handguns. The numbers of white men who are subject to such treatment could be counted on an abacus.

Fear spread to the liberal Democratic side of the table from time to time when Hillary had a bad week and Trump a good one – happily, a diminishing feature of the race. The question surfaced: what would be the consequences if he actually won the presidency?

Here psephology – lovely word and action: the science of elections – and dark forebodings confront each other. Psephologically, Trump cannot win on white voters. There are not enough of them on the shaky Republican side to carry it off. He has made little headway with Latino and none with African American voters. He is widely disliked by white women, a key and reliable voting group. It would take an unprecedented wave of new voters to sweep him into 1600 Pennsylvania Avenue. Thankfully, Trump believes in the Great Man Theory of History and refuses to prepare for debates, and disputes with those who try to prepare him. "Let Trump be Trump" is the best news for the Democrats.

If, however, the election outcome is close and Hillary emerges as the victor with a slender majority in the Electoral College, then Trump, always a sore loser and in this case a "yooge" one, would certainly resort to the courts to have the result overturned, and the rigged system that put Crooked Hillary in the White House exposed. It could be long, drawn-out, an ugly spectacle and damaging to the Republic.

Patrick McCaughey

Gary Werskey

In *Enemy Within* Don Watson writes with his customary blend of affection, wit, insight and style about American politics. He also displays a degree of critical empathy for the United States sadly lacking in the work of many other Australian pundits. As an American-Australian citizen, I highly value and appreciate these qualities.

However, if Watson still believes that the United States remains "the last great hope of humankind," then he has provided a devastating benchmark for just how low our world has ebbed. Indeed, towards the end of his essay, he appears to affirm the late John Updike's lament that his country was – already in the late 1980s – afflicted with a deep "malaise." Almost three decades later one can only imagine Updike elegantly turning in his grave at how the malaise has so dramatically morphed into the malady of this year's bewildering and dispiriting presidential election.

Don's instincts to try to make sense of the schizophrenic Clinton–Trump contest by focusing on Wisconsin are absolutely spot-on. On the one hand, much of the state has been for well over a century the centre of US progressive politics, and in some parts – not least its capital, Madison – still is. On the other, it has elected in recent years the corrupt ultra-conservative governor Scott Walker, as well as Mitt Romney's running mate and Republican powerbroker, Paul Ryan. These divided loyalties were manifested in 2012, when Obama carried Wisconsin by a comfortable seven points (still a drop from his victory there in 2008 by thirteen points). But when you drill down into the 2012 results you note that in the white suburban counties that ring Milwaukee, Romney outpolled Obama two to one. This is the same territory that Trump immediately entered to fuel white angst and anger in the wake of a shooting in downtown Milwaukee. While in mid-October Clinton leads Trump by an average of six points statewide, Wisconsin remains, like the rest of the country, a strongly polarised polity.

How did it come to this? My take is profoundly informed by my formation as the member of a staunchly Democratic family brought down by the Depression and then lifted up by FDR's New Deal. Despite being an army brat who moved around the world, my centre of gravity was and still is the Midwest – and, more particularly, a small town in north-western Illinois close to the Wisconsin border, where I spent most of my boyhood summers with my mother's parents. As it turned out, Wisconsin has figured quite often at critical moments in my (and my country's) political evolution. Here then are four very short personal stories from or about Badgerland to add to Don's collection.

My first political memory (age nine) arose from a family holiday in the summer of 1952, when my grandparents hired a rustic cabin nestled in the beautiful Wisconsin Dells. One night we gathered round the radio to listen to Adlai Stevenson's speech accepting the Democratic nomination for president. We were moved – a bit like a good sermon in church – partly because of Adlai's wit and eloquence and partly because, as a former Illinois governor, he was our favourite son. His misfortune was to be running against the ultimate American war hero, General Eisenhower. Yet there was never any question that both my grandfather – a night watchman, World War I vet and American Legion stalwart – and my father – a World War II vet and US army captain then stationed in Germany – would remain "madly for Adlai" in both the 1952 and 1956 elections. However, fast-forwarding to 2016, I have to ask myself, "For whom would these proud veterans now vote?" Their demographic would put them firmly in the sights of the Trump camp, a ripe target for its mantra of wanting to "make America great again." Here, then, is the first example of how the world of American politics has been up-ended.

In 1960 Wisconsin came into view again for me when JFK decided to take on the far more liberal Minnesota senator Hubert Horatio Humphrey (HHH) in that state's Democratic primary. Catholic Kennedy's challenge was to demonstrate that he could defeat HHH in the latter's Protestant progressive heartland. (Robert Drew's pioneering fly-on-the-wall film Primary documented this epic contest.) JFK won narrowly, but only thanks to the votes of Milwaukee's Eastern European immigrant Catholics. From there Kennedy immediately went on to Indiana in the hope of showing himself to be more electable in this even less promising state. There I was waiting – the fearless editor of my high school paper with a less than convincing press card – to encounter him at an early morning press conference in the steel-making and still largely white city of Gary. I even managed to ask him a question about his position on the Taft–Hartley industrial relations act! If I can't remember his answer, it's probably because I was so easily overwhelmed by his charm and Jackie's otherworldly beauty. (Barack and Michelle would have something of the same effect on liberal Democrats nearly fifty years later.) But the broader point here is that the working-class whites who so readily voted for Kennedy and other far more liberal Democrats up until the '60s were soon taking flight from cities like Milwaukee and Gary to the surrounding suburbs, which are today considered Trump strongholds. This is another instance of how Updike's "malaise" has worked to the disadvantage of Democratic progressives (including myself as early as 1969, when I was assaulted by white thugs at a polling booth while campaigning for Gary's first black mayor).

Following LBJ's overwhelming defeat of Barry Goldwater in 1964, a group of moderate Republicans organised to take back control of their party from conservative insurgents. As Watson notes, they formed the Ripon Society, named for the Wisconsin town where the GOP had been founded more than a century earlier. One of their number was my former Northwestern debate partner (and native of Sheboygan, WI), who subsequently became a speechwriter in the Nixon White House. As Watergate threatened to cast a shadow on his own reputation, he was plucked from Washington by a scion of the East Coast Republican establishment and installed as the publisher of the *International Herald Tribune* in Paris. Three decades later I caught up with him again in Washington during the 2008 presidential primary season. Over dinner with some of his well-placed Republican mates, he was asked which of the party's candidates he would be supporting, to which he replied without hesitation, "None of them!" As for the Democratic contenders, he cheerfully confessed that he would be happy to vote for "All of them!" When I emailed him this year about how Trump was viewed within his networks, he admitted he had yet to meet anyone who supported his party's nominee. So the "malaise" has also been at work in tearing apart the Republican Party and propelling it into unknown and troubling waters.

My final Wisconsin story arises from Watson's reference to one of my academic heroes, the University of Wisconsin's great radical American diplomatic historian William Appleman Williams. I read his classic *The Tragedy of American Diplomacy* (1959) in my final year at Northwestern, and its trenchant analysis of how much the pursuit of empire had shaped the United States certainly influenced my decision to oppose the Vietnam War in 1965. Two years later I brought this perspective into my work as a temporary staffer for a young Democratic congressman, Lee Hamilton, just into his second term, courtesy of Johnson's landslide victory in 1964. Hamilton sat on the House Foreign Affairs

Committee and its Southeast Asian subcommittee. Despite his great intelligence and goodwill, none of my arguments and references was going to budge him from his support of the war engineered by defence secretary Robert McNamara. This intellectual rebuff weighed less on me than the emotional toll registered several times a week in his office as we received the Department of Defense's notices of the servicemen from his district who had died in action.

However, one experience from this period that kept me tethered for a little while longer to the Democratic cause was sitting in a room with twenty or so other young staffers listening to Senator Robert F. Kennedy talk informally about his growing opposition to the war and his increasingly radical views about the causes and effects of social injustice inside the United States. The impact of his saddened, serious, intense authenticity on all of us was tangible in the moment, powerful in the knowledge that he was about to challenge Johnson for the Democratic nomination, and truly poignant in retrospect, given that he had less than a year to live. Along with Martin Luther King's assassination shortly thereafter, it seemed there was nowhere else for a liberal Democrat like me to go except further to the left and ultimately out of the party altogether. We became part of the ongoing tragedy of American diplomacy and yet another facet of Updike's malaise, thoroughly alienated from the Democratic establishment and profoundly doubtful that America any longer could lay claim to being humankind's last great hope.

Fifty years later, now that Bernie Sanders (our latest last great hope) has been sidelined, we and Wisconsin are left with a choice between the continuing more or less competent management of America's empire/tragedy – by Hillary and the Clinton-era economic and diplomatic apparatchiks who dominated the Obama years – and the void/abyss of a Trump presidency, which can only drive America's malaise into even deeper levels of violence and distress. And it will not only be US citizens who will bear the consequences of this choice. One can only hope that we in Australia will be ready to reappraise the American alliance unsentimentally in the light of our great and powerful friend's demons and frailties, as well as the strengths of its progressive forces past and present. Meanwhile, on Wisconsin – you bet!

Gary Werskey

Don Watson

The enemy of *Enemy Within* is not Donald Trump, but the fear and rancour at work in the United States, and the deep fractures that this election campaign has exposed. It's the "malaise" besetting the country: its roots are too old and deep to say with any confidence that we're really speaking of decline. I set out with no clear idea, except to avoid the Clintonite liberal orthodoxy of New York or a rust-belt town where anti-Clintonism – or anti-nearly-everybody – prevails. I chose to go to Wisconsin because it had a reputation for progressive politics, and Bernie Sanders' success in the Democratic primary there seemed to say it was enduring. At the same time, I knew that Wisconsin's governor was an archetype of the modern Republican who, through re-districting, voter registration and anti-union measures, had transformed a state once famous for its "across the aisle" cohesion. I fancied I might learn more about what was going on in the election from exposure to this polarised opinion.

I found the old Wisconsin overlaid with the new: the new being Scott Walker's brand of reactionary politics, fuelled by the Koch brothers, talkback radio, the Tea Party, Christian evangelism and a reflexive and venomous hostility to anything that can be called liberal. Wisconsin, as a former state congressman told me – and Gary Werskey in this issue movingly affirms – is not the tolerant, temperate and progressive place it once was. And the change in Wisconsin is very like the change occurring across the country.

It is a massive conceit to write about a country, a state and an election on the strength of a fifteen-day visit. The generous responses to this essay therefore came first as a relief, and second as enlightenment. Naturally, I will not be taking issue with people who have not taken issue with me. Where they have added further evidence or argument in support of my general case, as Patrick McCaughey, David Goodman and Bruce Wolpe have, I can only be grateful. The same goes for their corrections. I think Goodman is right to say that Americans are no more divided on party lines than they have been throughout their history: though it is true that fewer voters now inhabit the unaligned middle, and that it has been the Republicans' malevolent strategy for more than two decades to reject all compromise and obstruct democratic ambitions, even if it means closing down the government, the Supreme Court or the economy.

I would rather Patrick Lawrence had not embarrassed me with the news that the remark about coffee and killing oneself cannot be attributed to Albert Camus (I feel like I have known all my life that he said it), but I am glad to know better; and gladder still for his gritty discourse on Tocqueville and the "soft despotism" of the neoliberal consensus. I had not made the connection before, but it is a near-perfect designation for the assumptions of the elites, not least the doctrinaire political correctness that Tea Partiers and Trump supporters find oppressive. So-called liberals for whom globalisation has been a liberating and enriching force live in a universe so distant from the millions for whom it has been a disaster, they seem incapable of understanding them, or of extending to them the tolerance that at other times they hold up as their defining value. If tolerance depends in some measure on empathy, the Democrats should have it in abundance: yet they have little apparent capacity to put themselves in the shoes of those who see them as smug, corrupt, self-serving and deeply favoured by the system – and even less capacity, of course, to recognise their own failings. Give the Democrats the equivalent of the Clinton emails and they would be ruthless. Give them the Podesta emails and the tapes that indicate calculated and systemic disruption of Trump rallies and which received about a minute's media coverage, while Trump's eleven-year-old "sex tape" dominated the news for a week or more, and their outrage would be deafening. And yet, to listen sometimes, one would think they cast stones only after an internal audit has assured them that they are without sin.

Dennis Altman, I take it, would have had me write more – and more favourably – about Hillary Clinton; and less – and less favourably – about Bernie Sanders. More as well about why millions of Americans, including black Americans, like her so much. On that score I will excuse myself on the grounds that this support of the candidate is a given, and the essay is more concerned with what's at issue. However unfair the reasons might be, Hillary Clinton is one of the reasons the election has been so bitter. She's been part of the problem. That's why Sanders won Wisconsin and why he did well enough elsewhere to drag Clinton and the Democrats towards his more radical positions. It's why Trump was still doing so well deep into the campaign. As for my "bromance" with Bernie, like my "desperately" wanting to believe in the United States, I was not aware that my feelings ran so deep. Sometimes it's like that, I guess. Still, of all the candidates on both sides, Sanders did strike me as the most authentic, the most grounded, the most concrete in his speech and the one trying to make the electorate face up to some of the realities that are corroding the country (and helping Trump succeed), when Clinton was passing over them with "pragmatic progressive" bromides.

Thomas Jefferson thought a "temperate" mind was essential to democracy: his own (even at home on a plantation worked by slaves – with one of whom Thomas fathered six children) gave glorious expression to the idea that "all Men are created equal, that they are endowed by their creator with certain inaliena-ble rights ..." etc. Jefferson was a wonder of a human being and one of mighty contradictions. And so is the United States a wonder and full of contradictions – some of them, as H.L. Mencken insisted, are a consequence of Jeffersonian doctrine. Jefferson conceived of liberty, Mencken said, as freedom from the tyr-anny of a monarch. What he failed to recognise, but his rival Alexander Hamilton saw clearly, was the other necessary guarantee of democracy, namely freedom from the tyranny of the majority. So savage is this election, it seems possible that the people contesting it believe it will decide which majority can tyrannise the other for the next four years. Perhaps that's the case with all US elections, but surely the sense of it is more profound this year.

Jefferson would have loathed Donald Trump, of course. Trump is intemperate. Worse, he is vulgar. No breeding, manners or enlightened reasoning restrain him. There are no contradictions in Trump. He is all id, as some elements of the country are, as we all are now and then. Trump is the unrestrained part of the United States. In worshipping him, the unrestrained – or those who would be – are worshipping themselves, within the cult of freedom and ignorance of which they are honorary members. The rest are merely obsessed with him. In morbid fascination Americans now watch his fall as they did his rise, with barely a thought for the content of his policies. It's not his critique, but the manner of it that is so ... seductive.

His opponents, perhaps mindful of Jefferson, might like to pretend there's something un-American about Trump, but he's as apple-pie as any on either side of politics. He's the unapologetic go-getter; the Yankee bounder; the chancer; the champion of the deal; the great manipulator. He's the populist; the anti-intellec-tual, the rugged individualist; the people's friend; and the enemy of the elites. He's Barry Goldwater (for his racism) and LBJ (for his vulgarity) in one; he's Dr Stran-gelove and General MacArthur; P.T. Barnum, Ed Sullivan and Hugh Hefner. He's the ringmaster of celebrity, sex and fame. He takes what is his: and his is whatever he can take. In the lost world he promises to restore, this is the code they lived by.

What in some places is now called "inappropriate" behaviour was then called doing what comes naturally, and in Trumpland it still is. The intemperate Trump is no less the genuine American article than the temperate Clinton is.

As Nicole Hemmer amply demonstrates in her comment on the essay, not the least of Trump's Americanness is his anti-democratic tendency. She quotes the example of the Roosevelts, and of the populists Coughlin and Long, but we might add dozens of congressmen and senators, state governors, mayors, military men, sheriffs and small-town bosses – of varying degrees of corruption (which, if it is ever proved against Trump, will also be nothing new). To these, we could add any number of characters in popular culture. The anti-democratic thread in American life is as old as the democracy itself. And so is the corruption.

Hillary Clinton may lack her husband's political genius, but she could hardly have done better in this campaign. Her courage may one day become legendary. In those dreadful debates she returned Trump's brutal attacks on her character with much deadlier attacks on his, and deployed her temperate mind to beckon wavering voters with flawlessly marshalled facts and arguments. Not that the media or those who watch are judging the quality of her arguments, much less the content. In keeping with media practice, that she remains in charge of herself is enough: the products of that mind, such solutions to the country's problems as she might suggest, the policies she offers, are of no great interest.

If you think this overstates the case, just tune in to any of the networks (and dare to wonder if this might be the future in Australia). And if you will forgive such a crude conspiracy theory, the failure of the media networks to bring temperate minds to bear on policy and the rise and seeming fall of Donald Trump have the same cause – ratings, or, if you like, commerce. At a Kennedy School forum on 19 October, the NBC pollster Peter Hart was asked, "How do you understand the role of the media in this election cycle?" He replied:

> I think the one thing we can all agree on is, ratings have driven this. I mean, Donald Trump has been a magnet, I mean, in that you can put him on anytime, anywhere and bingo. I love sort of the "Morning Joe" element. You know, they created him, and then essentially, he turned on them, and they turned on him, and you know, you have all of this.

If Donald Trump is a squalid reminder of the dark side in American life, the country's media cannot escape the same judgment. If he's a joke and an embarrassment to the democracy conceived in liberty and defended in blood, ditto.

And if the substance of the policy choices has drawn minimal focus on any of the networks, ditto again. But if media ratings reflect public demand, most responsibility has to fall on the audience.

That was the point Richard Ford was making when he wrote about the malaise. John Updike's observations twenty years before him, Jimmy Carter's a decade or so before that, and the fascist United States Philip Roth imagined in 2004 conceived of the malaise in different ways, but all of them plant responsibility at the door of the democracy itself. Blame materialism, greed, cartels, intrigues, indifference, ignorance, xenophobia, fear, religious manias, unlikely sexual pathologies or intemperate minds – the country has flaws and lunacy in abundance: they are always there, waiting for a demagogue to stir them into something dire. It is the remarkable achievement of the United States that the democracy has never succumbed, and continues to be, if only after a fashion, the one revolution that ever worked. So far, that is.

Don Watson

Dennis Altman is a professorial fellow in human security at La Trobe University. His most recent books are *Queer Wars* (with Jon Symons) and *How to Vote Progressive in Australia* (edited with Sean Scalmer).

David Goodman teaches American history at the University of Melbourne. He is the author of *Radio's Civic Ambition: American Broadcasting and Democracy in the 1930s*, and is working on a grassroots history of the debate in the United States about US entry into World War II.

Stan Grant is Indigenous affairs editor at the ABC and Chair of Indigenous Affairs at Charles Sturt University. He won the 2015 Walkley Award for coverage of Indigenous affairs and is the author of *The Tears of Strangers* and *Talking to My Country*.

Nicole Hemmer is an assistant professor at the University of Virginia's Miller Center and a research associate at the US Studies Centre at the University of Sydney. She is the author of *Messengers of the Right: Conservative Media and the Transformation of American Politics* and a columnist for *US News & World Report* and the *Age*.

Patrick Lawrence is foreign affairs columnist at the Nation. He was a correspondent abroad for many years, chiefly for the *Far Eastern Economic Review*, the *International Herald Tribune* and the *New Yorker*. His most recent book is *Time No Longer: Americans after the American Century* (Yale).

Patrick McCaughey, a former director of the National Gallery of Victoria, has lived and worked in the United States since 1988. He has published widely on modern and contemporary art.

Gary Werskey studied history at Northwestern and Harvard universities and taught at Edinburgh University and Imperial College before immigrating to Australia in 1987. He is an honorary associate in the Department of History, School of Philosophical and Historical Inquiry, University of Sydney and chairs the Blackheath History Forum.

Bruce Wolpe was on the Democratic staff in Congress in President Obama's first term. He is a supporter of Hillary Clinton's campaign. He is chief of staff to former prime minister Julia Gillard.

QUARTERLY ESSAY AUTO-RENEWING SUBSCRIPTIONS NOW AVAILABLE SUBSCRIBE to Quarterly Essay & SAVE up to 23% on the cover price

Enjoy free home delivery of the print edition and full digital access on the Quarterly Essay website, iPad, iPhone and Android apps.

Subscriptions: Receive a discount and never miss an issue. Mailed direct to your door.

- [ ] **1 year auto-renewing print and digital subscription*** (4 issues): $69.95 within Australia. Outside Australia $109.95
- [ ] **1 year print and digital subscription** (4 issues): $79.95 within Australia. Outside Australia $119.95
- [ ] **1 year auto-renewing digital subscription*** (4 issues): $34.95
- [ ] **1 year digital only subscription** (4 issues): $39.95
- [ ] **2 year print and digital subscription** (8 issues): $149.95 within Australia

Gift Subscriptions: Give an inspired gift.

- [ ] **1 year print and digital gift subscription** (4 issues): $79.95 within Australia. Outside Australia $119.95
- [ ] **1 year digital only gift subscription** (4 issues): $39.95
- [ ] **2 year print and digital gift subscription** (8 issues): $149.95 within Australia

All prices include GST, postage and handling. *Your subscription will automatically renew until you notify us to stop. Prior to the end of your subscription period, we will send you a reminder notice.

Please turn over for subscription order form, or subscribe online at **www.quarterlyessay.com**
Alternatively, call 1800 077 514 or 03 9486 0244 or email subscribe@blackincbooks.com

Back Issues: (Prices include GST, postage and handling.)

- ☐ **QE 1** ($15.99) Robert Manne *In Denial*
- ☐ **QE 2** ($15.99) John Birmingham *Appeasing Jakarta*
- ☐ **QE 3** ($15.99) Guy Rundle *The Opportunist*
- ☐ **QE 4** ($15.99) Don Watson *Rabbit Syndrome*
- ☐ **QE 4** ($15.99) Mungo MacCallum *Girt By Sea*
- ☐ **QE 6** ($15.99) John Button *Beyond Belief*
- ☐ **QE 7** ($15.99) John Martinkus *Paradise Betrayed*
- ☐ **QE 8** ($15.99) Amanda Lohrey *Groundswell*
- ☐ **QE 9** ($15.99) Tim Flannery *Beautiful Lies*
- ☐ **QE 10** ($15.99) Gideon Haigh *Bad Company*
- ☐ **QE 11** ($15.99) Germaine Greer *Whitefella Jump Up*
- ☐ **QE 12** ($15.99) David Malouf *Made in England*
- ☐ **QE 13** ($15.99) Robert Manne with David Corlett *Sending Them Home*
- ☐ **QE 14** ($15.99) Paul McGeough *Mission Impossible*
- ☐ **QE 15** ($15.99) Margaret Simons *Latham's World*
- ☐ **QE 16** ($15.99) Raimond Gaita *Breach of Trust*
- ☐ **QE 17** ($15.99) John Hirst *'Kangaroo Court'*
- ☐ **QE 18** ($15.99) Gail Bell *The Worried Well*
- ☐ **QE 19** ($15.99) Judith Brett *Relaxed & Comfortable*
- ☐ **QE 20** ($15.99) John Birmingham *A Time for War*
- ☐ **QE 21** ($15.99) Clive Hamilton *What's Left?*
- ☐ **QE 22** ($15.99) Amanda Lohrey *Voting for Jesus*
- ☐ **QE 23** ($15.99) Inga Clendinnen *The History Question*
- ☐ **QE 24** ($15.99) Robyn Davidson *No Fixed Address*
- ☐ **QE 25** ($15.99) Peter Hartcher *Bipolar Nation*
- ☐ **QE 26** ($15.99) David Marr *His Master's Voice*
- ☐ **QE 27** ($15.99) Ian Lowe *Reaction Time*
- ☐ **QE 28** ($15.99) Judith Brett *Exit Right*
- ☐ **QE 29** ($15.99) Anne Manne *Love & Money*
- ☐ **QE 30** ($15.99) Paul Toohey *Last Drinks*
- ☐ **QE 31** ($15.99) Tim Flannery *Now or Never*
- ☐ **QE 32** ($15.99) Kate Jennings *American Revolution*
- ☐ **QE 33** ($15.99) Guy Pearse *Quarry Vision*
- ☐ **QE 34** ($15.99) Annabel Crabb *Stop at Nothing*
- ☐ **QE 35** ($15.99) Noel Pearson *Radical Hope*
- ☐ **QE 36** ($15.99) Mungo MacCallum *Australian Story*
- ☐ **QE 37** ($15.99) Waleed Aly *What's Right?*
- ☐ **QE 38** ($15.99) David Marr *Power Trip*
- ☐ **QE 39** ($15.99) Hugh White *Power Shift*
- ☐ **QE 40** ($15.99) George Megalogenis *Trivial Pursuit*
- ☐ **QE 41** ($15.99) David Malouf *The Happy Life*
- ☐ **QE 42** ($15.99) Judith Brett *Fair Share*
- ☐ **QE 43** ($15.99) Robert Manne *Bad News*
- ☐ **QE 44** ($15.99) Andrew Charlton *Man-Made World*
- ☐ **QE 45** ($15.99) Anna Krien *Us and Them*
- ☐ **QE 46** ($15.99) Laura Tingle *Great Expectations*
- ☐ **QE 47** ($15.99) David Marr *Political Animal*
- ☐ **QE 48** ($15.99) Tim Flannery *After the Future*
- ☐ **QE 49** ($15.99) Mark Latham *Not Dead Yet*
- ☐ **QE 50** ($15.99) Anna Goldsworthy *Unfinished Business*
- ☐ **QE 51** ($15.99) David Marr *The Prince*
- ☐ **QE 52** ($15.99) Linda Jaivin *Found in Translation*
- ☐ **QE 53** ($15.99) Paul Toohey *That Sinking Feeling*
- ☐ **QE 54** ($15.99) Andrew Charlton *Dragon's Tail*
- ☐ **QE 55** ($15.99) Noel Pearson *A Rightful Place*
- ☐ **QE 56** ($15.99) Guy Rundle *Clivosaurus*
- ☐ **QE 57** ($15.99) Karen Hitchcock *Dear Life*
- ☐ **QE 58** ($19.99) David Kilcullen *Blood Year*
- ☐ **QE 59** ($19.99) David Marr *Faction Man*
- ☐ **QE 60** ($22.99) Laura Tingle *Political Amnesia*
- ☐ **QE 61** ($22.99) George Megalogenis *Balancing Act*
- ☐ **QE 62** ($22.99) James Brown *Firing Line*
- ☐ **QE 63** ($22.99) Don Watson *Enemy Within*

☐ I enclose a cheque/money order made out to Schwartz Publishing Pty Ltd.
☐ Please debit my credit card (Mastercard, Visa or Amex accepted).

Card No. ☐☐☐☐ ☐☐☐☐ ☐☐☐☐ ☐☐☐☐

Expiry date / **CCV** **Amount $**

Cardholder's name **Signature**

Name

Address

Email **Phone**

Post or fax this form to: Quarterly Essay, Reply Paid 90094, Carlton VIC 3053 / Freecall: 1800 077 514
Tel: (03) 9486 0288 / Fax: (03) 9011 6106 / Email: subscribe@blackincbooks.com
Subscribe online at **www.quarterlyessay.com**